THE PASSENGER
A Mystery Novel

by

Donald W. Goodwin, M.D.
and
Walter H. Gunn, PhD

Wings Publications
Shawnee Mission, Kansas
1998

THE PASSENGER
A Mystery Novel

WINGS PUBLICATIONS
P.O. Box 161
U.S.A.
Mission, Kansas 66201

THE PASSENGER
A Mystery Novel
Goodwin, Donald W.
Gunn, Walter H.

Library of Congress catalog card No, 98-090178
ISBN 0-9618817-2-0

Airline mystery novel 2. Bomb Threat 4. Search 5. Takeoff 6. Washington and Omaha 13. Six Hours Out 14. Dulles Epilogue, Note on Explosives

First Printing

Printed by Walsworth Publishing Company
Marceline, Missouri 64658 USA

Donald W. Goodwin, M.D., is University Distinguished Professor
Emeritus of Psychiatry at Kansas University. He has written more than a
dozen books, including Anxiety, Is Alcoholism Hereditary? and Alcohol
and the Writer. The paperback edition of the latter book was released by
Penguin. It won The Society of Midland Authors Prize and was praised by
illustrious people such as Karl Menninger:

"One of the most interesting books by a fellow psychiatrist
that I have ever read."

Captain Walt Gunn is a retired 747 pilot with 39 years of seniority with
TWA. He has a PhD in psychology and is an assistant Clinical Professor of
Psychiatry at the Kansas University Medial Center. He is Adjunct Professor
of Aviation at Central Missouri State University. He is author of The Joy of
Flying: Overcoming the Fear. His second book, A Life Aloft is now
available depicting his airline career from DC-3 to 747. He is often
consulted by the media, military, and airline industry when there are
concerns about human factors in aviation safety.

Cover design by
Ion Paleologue

THE PASSENGER

Table of Contents

Foreword

The people and events in this book are largely fictitious. There is no Transatlantic airline, for example. Roy Orbison was real. Also real are the airports, the mini-history of airplane bomb threats, the North Atlantic and of course the jumbo jet.

Prologue

On December 21, 1988, a bomb exploded on Pan American Flight 103 over Scotland, killing 277 people. The airline knew of the bomb threat, but did not warn the passengers.

On December 30, 1989, Northwest Airline Flight 51 flew safely from Paris to Detroit after receiving a bomb threat. Booked passengers were told of the threat and 22 boarded the plane while more than 100 changed flights.

On a gray day in June it happened again.

1

Boarding

The airport in Frankfurt is six miles from the city limits and a plane ride away from the major cities of the world. From hotel to airport it took 25 minutes by autobahn, for which the cab driver received 35 marks. A small man emerged, clutching a carry-on bag. The driver produced a larger bag from the trunk. Carrying both, the small man walked toward the entrance.

Abruptly he turned around. "Hold on there!" he said, and walked back to the cab. "Aha!" he said, reaching through the window and retrieving a hat. A large hat for a small man. Scruffy brown. A cowboy hat.

He put the hat on his head and started back for the entrance. Two armed guards flanked the glass doors. Their eyes grazed over him and moved on to the others. Inside, he turned right into the international area. Reaching the check-in counter involved negotiating his way through a crowd of travelers. A cosmopolitan lot: turbans and tennis shoes, beards of all varieties, clean-shaven business types, women and children. The noise matched the varied dress styles: a babble of voices in a variety of languages punctuated by public address announcements in English, German, French and occasional third-world dialects.

As he approached the Transatlantic counter, the crowd thinned out. He found himself facing a bank of check-in counters, each with a fresh-faced man or woman in a navy blue jacket peering from behind. Each looked puzzled, distracted, worried, or some combination.

All were idle. There was not a single passenger in front of the six counters.

The man with the cowboy hat passed up the first-class counter and walked up to the third of the five tourists counters. He handed over his ticket envelope and passport.

The young woman accepted them with a breathy sigh that could have expressed satisfaction or anything. She spread out the tickets, looked down, looked up, said:

"Dulles?"

"Dulles."

At this point, check-in agents usually start punching their computers to confirm the reservation, but not this time. Instead she looked hard at her passenger with the cowboy hat and asked, "Were you called?"

"About the bomb? They reached me at the Hilton."

"And you are going?"

"Sure. Why not?"

She paused and looked around as if for a supervisor.

"Well," she said. "It's downright strange." From the accent she could have been from Texas. "Do you know something, mister? You're it."

"I am it?"

"It. You are the only one going."

The small man with the big hat looked thoughtful, then smiled.

"But there have been other threats. Most people have flown anyway."

"Not this time. One hundred seventy seven people had reservations. There have been a bunch of cancellations. The flight leaves in an hour, or was supposed to. You're our only passenger so far."

Again, she looked right and left. "Maybe somebody else will show up," she said. "It doesn't look that way."

The passenger shrugged, removed his hat and said, "What should I do?"

"That's a good question. Right now we don't know whether 131 is flying or not. Ah, good."

A middle-aged woman with a carnation in her coat lapel said, "So somebody showed up. What have you told him?"

"That we don't know whether it's flying."

"That's true. What is your preference, sir?"

"Well, it may fly. Is that right? I've checked. It's my only chance of getting to Washington today."

The three looked at each other. The supervisor said, "OK, knowing what you know, go on through. If the flight is cancelled, it will show up on the announcement board."

She smiled. "In your case, I suspect you will be paged and get the news personally."

❦

There was a long line at the X-ray machine and metal detector. Between check-in and security—some 30 yards apart—he saw three uniformed guards carrying short-nosed automatic rifles. Laying his carry-on on the X-ray conveyor belt, he saw a German shepherd a few feet to the right, held on a leash by a guard. He walked through the metal detector.

"Please empty your pockets." The guard was pleasant enough, in a way paranoids are sometimes pleasant.

The pockets produced some small change, billfold, a plastic comb, nail clipper and a handkerchief as large as a bandanna. Everything went into a red plastic bowl and the small man re-entered the metal detector.

"Coins would do it," the friendly guard said as the passenger re-pocketed everything from the bowl.

Tugging his carry-on off the conveyor belt, he turned and walked squarely into a long table. Standing behind the table were four men in suits and sports jackets, poking into small luggage and handbags while their owners waited with tight lips except when interrogated. He dumped his carry-on on the table and sat his cowboy hat beside it. A man with a seamed face and gray curly hair looked at him and then the bag.

"Where are you going?" He had a German accent.

"The U.S. Dulles."

"Where have you been in Europe?"

"Just Frankfurt."

"Why were you in Frankfurt?"

"To visit a friend."

"What is the friend's name."

"Julie Goudet."

"Spell that please."

The interrogator wrote down the name.

"When did you arrive in Frankfurt?" The interrogator thumbed through the passenger's passport as he asked questions and listened.

"Four days ago. I flew directly from Kennedy."

"And live in Omaha, Nebraska?"

"I flew from Omaha to Kennedy."

6

"What do you do for a living?"

"Doctor. Chest surgeon."

The interrogator had turned the hat over and was peering into the crown. He turned it around and ran a finger through the band.

"Tell me about your friend."

"She's a doctor too. We met in Omaha. She works just south of here at the Rhein-Main Air Base."

"What kind of work?"

"I really don't know. She's not allowed to talk. Not medicine, I gather. Something confidential."

For the first time the interrogator looked interested.

"Confidential?"

"Yes. You know, secret. She really won't talk about it."

"Is she German?"

"Half. Her father was French. She got her M.D. from Stuttgart. Came to Omaha to do a radiology residency."

The interrogator frowned and rubbed his nose. "Why is a doctor working in an air force base? You must have some idea."

"Well, I knew she had friends at SAC—the strategic air command base—in Omaha. She may have moonlighted in the hospital on the SAC base. That's really all I know."

"Lovers?"

The little man did not respond.

"Married?"

He still did not respond.

"Ever been arrested?" came next, followed by several questions about drug use, gambling and acquaintances from the Middle East.

He opened the carry-on and explored its contents with nicotine-stained fingers, removing nothing.

"OK, Mr. Corrigan, go on through."

Another line formed at Passport Control, but it moved quickly. The man in the cubicle looked at the passport, and passed it through the window. His boredom seemed as permanent as his skewed tie.

The departure lounge was half full. People stood, walked, sat. A few sat on the floor., backs to wall. Some napped. Travel detritus was strewn

everywhere: bags, plastic sacks, Coke cans, coffee dregs in plastic cups.
Corrigan shuffled closer to the enormous black announcement board.
One-thirty-one was scheduled to depart at 13:50. Where most flights said
"On Time," TA 131 said "Delay."

It was now 12:31.

❧

In the next three hours and forty-five minutes, Corrigan did the following:

He found a seat as far from other travelers as possible. For one hour
and forty minutes he stared alternately at the announcement board and a
dog-eared paperback he had produced from his carry-on. An observer
might have judged him a slow reader. In that time, he didn't turn a page.

He strolled through the duty-free shops, a supermarket of luxuries
coveted by many and affordable by few. In the liquor store he bought a
liter of Johnny Walker Black that would be delivered later to him on the
plane. Money calculations seemed as important to the shoppers as the
goods.

He went to the men's room.

He bought a Herald-Tribune. He bought a beer. He took both to a table
where he could see the announcement board. He sipped beer and read—
actually seemed to read—the back page of the Herald-Trib. Once he
grinned slightly. Art Buchwald is often on the back page.

"May I join you?"

A dapper, youngish man with red hair stood next to the table, holding
a Danish in one hand, a coffee cup in the other.

Corrigan nodded and turned to the sports page.

"Where are you headed?"

Corrigan saw the man was wearing a tan official-looking jacket.
Clipped to the pocket was a name tag with a picture.

"Washington, D.C. Sure, sit down."

Sitting, the man said, "I guess your flight's delayed."

Corrigan nodded and waited.

"Bomb threat."

"So I hear."

"Reason for the delay. Has to be. All those dogs sniffing luggage.
Trouble getting through security?"

8

"Not really."

"Old-fashion magnetometer, metal detector to most. Heathrow and DeGaulle have neutron units, TNAs. Huge affairs. Pick up plastic."

Corrigan said, "I went through one at Kennedy. It reminded me of an MRI standing on end."

"MRI?"

"Magnetic Resonance Imaging. Every hospital has one."

"And you work at hospitals?"

"Yes." Corrigan had a resigned look. "I'm a physician. Chest surgeon."

"Oh. You know, this whole ramp area is called sterile, like an operating room. Passengers are sterile once they go through security. People who work here are sterile."

He looked down at his name tag. "We all wear these. That's to let everyone know we are sterile."

Corrigan said, "But you still have children." The red-haired man grinned. "Want to hear a funny story?"

Not waiting for answer: "There was an airline pilot who walked through sterile areas in airports all around Europe wearing his name tag. He did this for two years before someone noticed the picture was of a dog."

❦

At 16:15 a light went on next to TA 131 and the sign said Boarding, Gate V165. Corrigan took the escalator to the lower level. A customer service agent—boutonniered, blue jacket—seemed to recognize him.

"Mr. Corrigan? Over here, please."

He followed the agent down the corridor to a door.

"The tram will be here shortly," the agent said. Indeed it was. A guard opened the door. Corrigan walked outside and saw the tram: a streetcar with rubber wheels in two sections joined by accordion pleats.

The tram door opened and he climbed aboard. No one preceded him on the tram; no one followed. After a time the door shut and the tram rolled away across the tarmac. There was just Corrigan and the driver.

❦

The Frankfurt terminal is a sprawling, multi-level, stark gray marble, concrete and glass building, a major hub for European airlines and inter-

9

national air carriers. Adjoining the airport on the south is the Rhein-Main Air Base serving the United States Air Force and German Aviation Authority.

Sightseers can see planes land and take off by looking through a high chain-link fence or from an observation deck atop the major terminal. From the observation deck one gazes on a kaleidoscope of colors: logos and stylized paint schemes of the arriving and departing planes scattered along more than a mile of parking ramps.

The day was a little nippy for June. Wind blew in gusts across the top of the deck. Foliage around the parking lot north of the terminal was green, but the sky was lead gray and rain seemed likely.

A woman with long brown hair and a green coat stood alone on the observation deck. The hair blew in the wind. She was looking through a swivel telescope that cost twenty pfennig to operate for five minutes.

Through it she saw a tram with accordion pleats move slowly toward the outer reaches of the parking area. Standing alone, humpbacked and forlorn, was a 747 parked as far away from the terminal as a plane could park.

Where it was parked was called Gate V165, but there was no gate. As a fish might nose up to a whale, the tram stopped by the plane. She saw a man leave the tram and walk across the tarmac to a stairway leading up to an open door in the plane's flank.

The man climbed the stairway. He entered the door. A moment later the door closed.

He was the only passenger.

2

Threat

John McCabe was not in his office when the phone rang. He was in the bathroom. There was a phone in the bathroom. "Yes."

"Frankfurt calling."

It wasn't Frankfurt. It was the dispatcher from Kennedy calling about Frankfurt. McCabe was in his Rockefeller Plaza office. There early, as always.

"Trouble," the dispatcher said.

"Put him on."

Now he was talking both to the dispatcher and the Frankfurt district manager on an international phone hookup.

"Air Cargo again?" McCabe asked.

"Right. How did you know?"

"Bomb threats in New York often come to Air Cargo first. It's first in the Yellow Pages." McCabe paused. "But Air Cargo is not first in the Yellow Pages in Frankfurt," he added.

"That's right. German for air is flug. He called flug whatever-the-word-is. So much for alphabet."

"And what did he say?" McCabe was Vice President of Flight Operations for Transatlantic, responsible for everything that flew.

"Bang. Don't fly one-thirty-one tomorrow or else. Hold on. Looking at my notes. The guy in Air Cargo—flug whatever—called and I had trouble understanding him. His English isn't too hot."

Nor was the station manager's German. He was from Philadelphia and had been in Frankfurt six weeks. Misassignment, some said.

The operations VP and dispatcher knew the new Frankfurt station manager. His name was Abe. Abe had been with the company for twenty-three years. The three had gotten a little drunk once after a meeting.

Now Interpol joined them on the hookup. He sounded British. Public school British.

"We called the FBI and airport police. The caller wants to blow up one-three-one tomorrow. Give us fifteen minutes and we'll have the passenger list."

The dispatcher said, "It's Friday. People leave early."

"What'er you talking about. It's not even seven New York time. We'll get it there, half an hour at most."

The man from Interpol, speaking from his basement office at Frankfurt airport, had not given his name. Just Interpol. McCabe was annoyed.

"What's your name, Interpol?"

"John, same as yours."

"Dandy. Call me McCabe."

"Okay, McCabe. Let's go through it. Guy in Air Cargo gets the call at noon Frankfurt time. Confused. Calls Security. Security calls us, the FBI and airport cops. Really no delay."

"The message?"

"Well, that's a problem. The Air Cargo guy got flustered. Didn't take it down. The caller was a man. He called at 12:05."

"You said noon."

"Sorry. Rounding off."

"Please, don't round off."

Interpol didn't know the operations chief, but he knew the tone of voice. He also knew the type.

"Five handicapper?"

"What in the hell does that mean?"

"Sorry. Nothing. Let's get on with it."

McCabe wondered how Interpol knew he was a five handicapper. Bastards got around. Or did he fit a profile? Interpol was big on profiles.

"Everything at the airport okay?" McCabe asked.

"Abe said sure. Interpol said absolutely. Security people would be watching, but until tomorrow, toward flight time, that really just meant watching. Eyes open."

There was a checklist for bomb threats. McCabe looked through it.

"Air Cargo have anything else besides the message? Background noises?

Abe answered. "He thought the call came from an airport. Thought he heard planes taking off. We're not sure. He hears planes taking off all the time. Jesus, that's where he works. May or may not have been over the phone." He added, "Guy's got bad English."

"Anything else?"

"Well, yes. Beware of plastic. He said somebody might have some plastic. He said watch out. Then he hung up."

"Plastic. They all say plastic. Every nut knows about plastic."

"Right. We don't have a TNA at Frankfurt," Abe said.

"Next year, we hope," McCabe said. TNA picked up plastic.

Interpol: "Anyway, the passenger list goes to Washington in an hour or so." (McCabe thought: fifteen minutes, half hour, now hour or so.) "Usual routine. Passports. FBI. Keep the computers busy."

McCabe was looking at tomorrow's flight schedule. Nearly four hundred TA flights flew domestic and oversees daily. The airline had become big domestically a year or so ago after the junk-bond takeover.

There was about one bomb threat a week. The operations chief was used to being called in his bathroom.

But he was always fresh, always concerned. He had flown commercial planes. He had a chunk of tail rip off in a lightning storm. He could empathize.

It was a waiting game. The computer at passport would check the passengers for suspects. J. Edgar Hoover—McCabe's name for the FBI—would do arrests, convictions, less savory FBI stuff. Interpol had a list of terrorists, where they were located (maybe). "Terrorists" was a broad term. It could include a Palestinian kid caught on camera shaking his fist.

"What about the press?" the district manager asked. "Shit," McCabe said. "The goddamn press. Someone sets a precedent and we're stuck with it."

"The phone's going to ring any minute," Abe said, and was right. The others could hear the phone ring in his Frankfurt airport office. Abe told somebody to wait a minute.

3

Boarding

An American airline crew, arriving in Frankfurt, Germany, at 9:05 a.m. after losing a night's sleep, had two choices: shop or go to bed. Donaldson chose bed.

His wife, Susan, who came with him whenever she could, chose shopping. They split in the Mainz Hotel lobby. Susan and two other hostesses headed for the shops. It was Friday, a busy shopping day. Donaldson took the elevator to his room.

Twenty-four years of flying international and he still had jet lag. The women were wide awake; some may have napped during the in-flight movie. He follows his established routine: hot tub bath, force himself to sleep four or five hours, force himself awake, shower, dress casually, go for a walk.

He had been married to Susan for six months. He hated to face it but had been relieved when she went shopping. She interfered with his routine. Okay, nicely interfered. He needed the routine to sleep that night. She understood and didn't understand. She could go 48 hours without sleep and not seem to miss it. Or sometimes, when they arrived at the hotel, she hopped into bed and slept straight through to breakfast. He couldn't predict which she would do and it made him edgy.

He was 52, she was 36. He hoped this wasn't the problem. His divorce had come through two years ago. He had met her on a flight from New York to London. She had brought continental breakfasts to the cockpit an hour before landing. She had asked how far the hotel was from Harrod's.

Waiting beside her for the bus, he half-whispered, "Was going to Harrod's myself. Wanna tag along?"

So it began.

Susan was to join him that evening at a gasthaus near the hotel. She

14

was late. Donaldson sat on a bar stool and sipped a beer. The rule was: no drinking on layovers. Donaldson would have another beer—maybe two—with his eisbein mit sauerkraut. It cut the salt and fat. Others from the crew, besides Susan, might join him, and might have a beer too. They were a little careful about where they drank—certainly avoiding tourist places—but nobody made trouble. There was an old air crew saying: Beer is food in Germany.

It was nearly midnight, still Friday, when the Donaldsons arrived back at the hotel. Donaldson was bushed. He had danced like a teenager and hoped he hadn't looked foolish, but then thought who gives a damn.

The red light on the telephone blinked. The station manager told Donaldson about the bomb threat.

❦

They had arrived on Friday morning and now it was Saturday morning. The bomb threat had come at noon Friday. As a result, crew call at the Mainz Hilton came an hour earlier, on Saturday.

The switchboard put the crew dispatcher through to eighteen crew members in their separate rooms.

"Good morning, sir or miss, whichever," he said in fractured English. "Leaving a little early today. Meet in the lobby at eleven."

"Why," a few asked.

"Captain will explain."

Donaldson didn't explain. He said they could talk about it on the bus. He didn't like lobby briefings. Passengers might eavesdrop.

The attendant named Linda looked paler than usual, but all boarded the bus: fifteen attendants—six men, nine women, from early twenties to late forties—co-pilot, flight engineer. Donaldson got on last. Susan had grabbed the front seat and he sat beside her. ("Let them talk," they had earlier decided.)

He had known some of the older attendants for years and recognized others but couldn't call them by name. The cockpit crew, a product of the monthly bidding for runs, stayed together for a month. The flight attendants formed and reformed in various combinations, although those from the domiciles (New York, Chicago and LA) often knew each other. Susan had traded with another attendant to make the Frankfurt run.

The bus was a 40-seater, plush, sightseeing transport with panoramic glass domes. Flight crews were jaded tourists with little appreciation of the comfort or scenery. Some dozed, other talked a little, conserving energy for the task ahead: eight to ten hours with demanding passengers, kids crying or running amok, a few drunks, foreign language problems and endless complaints, often about things that happened before the boarding ("I was overcharged by the cab driver. Can you do something?").

The jadedness was not so apparent today. Instead there was palpable apprehension.

The Mainz Hotel is a favorite for many American tourists. It's away from the big city hassle of Frankfurt. Quaint shops, gasthauses, parks and scenic areas along the river Main, not far from the confluence with the Rhein.

The bus moved slowly around the circle entry to the hotel and proceeded to the Autobahn spur for the Frankfurt Main Flughafen.

Seated forward, the Donaldsons had unobstructed views for the 30-minute ride as the bus entered the cleared opening in the forest-lined Autobahn. He turned to face the others.

"Okay, folks, yesterday there was a call. It was a bomb threat. Security has been on it all night and we'll know more when we get there. You know the new policy. The company is notifying everybody booked on the flight, let them change their plans if they want to. For now, we'll proceed through departure and hold briefing as usual." Donaldson paused, then continued.

"If anyone isn't happy with the situation, you can opt to deadhead home tomorrow. No problem. Now, sit back and enjoy the scenery."

Turning to Susan, he spoke softly. "I'm going straight to operations and get McCabe on the phone. Stay with the gang and as soon as I know more I'll come back for the briefing. Don't bother going to Duty Free. We don't need any booze this trip—plenty at home."

Muffled conversations of the crew blended into the rumbling tones of the road, disguising the content of their discussions, but not the uneasiness.

Bill McCoy was seated behind Donaldson and Susan. Leaning forward, he said, "Skipper, I'm going to the plane as soon as I clear departure. Want to look everything over."

"Okay with me. I'll join you as soon as I get New York straightened out on this. McCabe may have a wild hair." Donaldson's idea of wild hair: orders to ferry the plane back with just crew. "If it's not safe enough for passengers, I don't want to be on it," was Donaldson's philosophy. "Heroes in ivory towers need to be kept honest," he told McCoy. "Check things yourself. Don't know about kraut security in these situations."

Susan studied Ron's handling of things. Once more it confirmed her attraction to him. His confidence in command was infectious to his crews. It was exhilarating to Susan.

Nearing the airport turnoff, the driver slowly came to a halt. A lineup of traffic ahead. Polizei cars with the flashers blinking. Donaldson surveyed the number of cars blocking their progress. Movement ceased.

He signaled the driver to open the door. Donaldson's German was limited, the driver's English nil. Walking past the stalled cars, Ron went to the head of the line to inquire about the disruption. He was recognized in his uniform by one of the officers, who said, "Gutentag Capitan."

"What's the holdup?" Ron asked. "We're running late."

The officer's English was intelligible. "There is a security plan. We inspect autos for entry to the airport. We'll try to help."

"I can vouch for the passengers. All crew members. We're on TA 131 and must report in about ten minutes."

"I will have Corporal Plapp examine your bus and escort you mach schnell, Herr Capitan."

"Ja, verstehen. Danke Schon," Ron replied in his college German. The Corporal was told to accompany Herr Capitan to the bus.

Corporal Plapp walked through the bus, flipping through each passport after comparing the photo with the seated crew member. Satisfied, he stepped out of the bus and signaled the driver around the line of cars. As they neared the airport entry, traffic slowed with the congestion of vehicles delivering passengers for the rush of mid-day departures.

Donaldson and McCoy walked quickly through the lobby. Each had his personal bag and flight kit. Donaldson's bag, circa World War II, was good for packing everything he needed, however long the trip.

McCoy was proud of his two-suiter aluminum Halliburton with twenty-two years of banging around and tamper-proof locks he had jerryrigged. He never did hear from the factory on his patent proposal—Halliburton's loss.

As uniformed crew members with photo IDs in view, they entered the employees' security doors, placed their bags on the X-ray conveyor, stepped through the emergency magnetometer archway and claimed their bags.

"Excuse me, Captain," the uniformed guard spoke. "We are inspecting all bags now. Would you please open them for our look?"

"Not at all, I understand."

Both opened their bags, McCoy fumbling with his locks. Each flipped open their flight kits and stood back.

The security officer felt through the clothing in each bag with an obvious effort to avoid leaving the items in disarray.

"Thanks you, Captain. Guten tag."

Donaldson led the way. They went down the employee elevator to TA station operations on ramp level. Abe Steiner, TA's station manager, greeted Donaldson and McCoy, inviting them to his private office. McCabe, in New York, was waiting for their call. McCabe was in the bathroom again. It was pre-dawn in New York.

"Ron, that you?"

"Just got to the airport. They're even checking cars coming off the Autobahn. Been on TV yet?"

"Yesterday. All day. The Feds and Interpol are in high gear."

"They think it's credible?"

"They're putting a lot of stock in the specificity criteria."

"Nothing fits the other two criteria?"

"Not so far. No disgruntled TA employees threatened their boss. No histories of violence."

"What did the caller say?"

"Not much. That's the point. 'Watch for plastic,' he said and hung up."

Donaldson commented, "He didn't say, 'Now you pay for everything—all will die—God wills it—fly and die?"

"No. He didn't rave. Just said the plane would be bombed and watch out for plastic. Crisp, to the point. Almost friendly. That's what is meant by 'specific.' Anyway, that's how Security reads it. So we're pulling out the stops."

"Okay, John, we'll do a number on 109."

(As Donaldson had once explained to his son, every plane is assigned a number that lasts its lifetime. Flight numbers change with flights. When pilots talk with ground airline personnel, they use the plane number. They use the flight number to air traffic and in timetables.)

(It might seem confusing, but isn't—not to pilots on the line and their company colleagues. Donaldson had arrived in Frankfurt Friday morning on TA plane 103. It was now Saturday and in three hours he was scheduled to head back to Dulles. He would be flying plane 109, a.k.a. flight 131, which had arrived three hours earlier from Dulles.)

Groundtime for a plane was incredibly expensive. Turnaround times for planes was as fast as possible. Layover time for crews was longer—this time, in Frankfurt, twenty-six hours.

"What do you think it will cost?" Donaldson asked. "Holding a 747 three hours for a bomb threat?"

"Maybe ten, twelve thou. A lot. No choice."

"Tell me, John, do we ever not check these days?"

"Sometimes. Depends on how credible the threat."

"If you call this one credible, you must call them all credible."

"Better to play safe, Ron."

"Agree. Anything else?"

"Not at the moment. I'll call you in a half hour or so."

"Got to brief the crew. Any ideas?"

"The truth, of course. Anybody seem antsy?"

"None so far. Everybody came from the hotel. I said they could make their decision after the briefing. Probably will lose a lot of passengers. What's the logic behind this gut-spilling to the public? We'll start having one every day! Crazy policy."

"I agree, Ron, but between the media, the Feds and our legal eagles, nobody will let us forget Pan Am 103. I can't see it working, but what can I do? Return to flying? Leave this desk job for the wimpy set? Might do it but I'm still one number behind you on the seniority sheets. Hate to see you outbid me on the plush runs."

Seniority was determined by age at date of hire. Donaldson was two months older and one number above McCabe in seniority. It might seem trivial but might also determine whether you flew on Christmas or stayed home with the wife and kids. It might also determine whether you were copilot if all the left hand seats were taken.

McCabe could see himself flying copilot with Donaldson in the Captain's seat. He groaned. It was too much to bear. McCabe wasn't really tempted.

❧

Seeing Susan in the briefing room, Donaldson thought of another layover lesson: Only eat when hungry. When hungry, eat breakfast, whatever the hour. Sleep when sleepy. Listen to your body.

In the three years he had known Susan the other layover lessons had gone to the wind. He still listened to his body, but his body told him different things now.

Susan in her uniform and pillbox hat was giving his body directions which he forced himself to ignore. Time to brief the crew.

"Okay, here's what we've got. A cargo handler in Frankfurt's air freight got a call about noon yesterday, Friday, saying there would be a bomb on the plane and watch for plastic. Apparently that's all he said. Security is taking it seriously. Mainly, I guess, because he said so little . . . not the usual garbage.

"New York has ordered a complete inspection. The plane from nose to tail, freight, a check on every passenger. It's already started. Probably be a three hour delay."

"Then we'll fly?" asked a middle-aged attendant who looked, and probably was, as tough as nails.

"That depends on New York. Right now they're waiting to see what, if anything, turns up."

They sat on chairs and lounges in a semicircle, looking at Donaldson, calmly standing, hands in pockets. There were no smiles, no joking.

"Let's assume they don't find anything," he said. "Assume we fly. Anybody want to stay here?"

Some looked straight ahead, deadpanned. Others looked furtively at the others. It was a painful moment—macho competing with caution, courage with the survival instinct. More than anything, there was the fear of looking weak. The wrong stuff.

One by one four attendants stood up. Three were women and one a man. One was Linda, paler than ever. Donaldson knew something about Linda no one else in the room probably knew. She was terrified of flying; she was an aerophobic, was seeing a psychologist in Washington. Forcing

20

herself to fly was a defense against the phobia—what the psychologists call a counterphobia. The counterphobia had just laid down and died.

Linda was neurotic. He felt sorry for her. Donaldson knew pilots who had a fear of heights: acrophobia. Flying planes didn't bother them, perhaps because the windows were so high and narrow they couldn't imagine falling out.

Donaldson didn't know the other three attendants. The man, he suspected, was gay. But gays were as brave as straights, in his experience. Maybe the fellow had met someone in the hotel.

"Fine," Donaldson said. "Look, don't worry about it. We can count on a reduced load. No bad marks for anyone, no problem. We'll put you on tomorrow's flight."

The four marched out of the room, looking straight ahead. Two of the women were about in tears.

A low murmur swept the room. The relief that comes from passing a test, making a tough decision, looking good.

Some might be visualizing a picture in the hometown newspaper. "Local heroine . . . " A tale of courage or a funeral announcement? The alternatives brought a shiver, a little regret, perhaps, about being so macho. The right stuff.

The rest was routine, predicated on flying.

Donaldson: "Weather enroute, good. Jet stream, turbulence off Newfoundland coast. Buckle up ten or fifteen minutes. Don't spill booze . . .

"Good ride to Dulles. Scattered thunderstorms. East coast needs the rain. Flying time 7:49.

"No traffic delays over there . . .

"The flight path will be over London, Dublin, Iceland, south tip of Greenland, then the Maritimes of Canada to offshore Boston, to Philadelphia, to Dulles.

"Any questions?"

There were none.

4

Search

Every large airport has an area set aside for bomb searches, but most don't give it a name. Frankfurt gives it a name: Bomb Search Area. It's shown on maps of the airport, west of the terminal, beyond the parking ramp, between two freight buildings.

Some years Frankfurt gets more bomb threats than any other airport.

The search of TA 131 began at 13:10, Saturday, 30 minutes before scheduled takeoff. The flight would be delayed, but no one could predict when a bomb might be planted. The last piece of luggage or freight put aboard might contain a bomb. The man in brown coveralls with the name tag who takes a final swipe of a toilet seat with a cleaning cloth may be a terrorist who outwitted Security.

Nobody could be sure.

Donaldson certainly couldn't be sure. Abe drove him to the search area in his Mercedes. The dozen or so inspectors had already started going over the plane.

McCoy, his flight engineer, was already there, starting his own inspection. Donaldson saw McCoy's fanny before he saw McCoy. The Flight Engineer was on his knees, heedless of the effect the oil-stained tarmac might have on his uniform trousers. His head was wedged between two giant tires, each separated from the axle by about eight inches. He was inspecting the disc brakes. This always amazed Donaldson when he saw it. McCoy had a narrow head. Cephalic Index around 60. Most people couldn't stick their head between the tires and the axle. They looked with a mirror.

A 747 is an 18-wheeler: two wheels on the nose gear, four wheels on each wing gear and four wheels on each body gear, arranged in tandem. Before he was through, McCoy might wedge his size 60 head between all nine sets.

He was very particular. He didn't trust anyone else looking at or fixing his airplane. His head emerged and he stood up.

"Good afternoon, Skipper." Donaldson and McCoy were friends but on duty it was Skipper, not Ron (or Captain, as the others called him).

"Guess what I know," said the Captain.

McCoy wiped his hands on a rag and waited.

"It's 30 minutes before scheduled departure. Less. Only one passenger has shown up."

"One?"

"It's incredible. Maybe they know something we don't."

"Does that mean the threat is more serious or less?" McCoy grinned.

"Dunno. Never happened before. To my knowledge."

"They should be getting hold of these passengers and find out why."

McCoy was thinking it over. "Creepy, isn't it? Does the rest of the crew know?"

"Nobody knew until an hour or so ago. Four attendants have said they aren't going."

"Hell, one passenger. They can all stay. Nice swimming pool at the Hilton."

Donaldson looked up at the sky. "If the sun comes out. Cold for June."

McCoy was right. One passenger. Who needed attendants? Donaldson would be happy personally to serve the guy (was it a guy?) a drink, peanuts, microwaved lunch, wine, microwaved snack. With the plane on autopilot and computerized navigation, he was hardly needed anyway.

One passenger. Strange, strange.

"Will we fly?" McCoy asked.

"Probably. Have to get the equipment back to the States. I'm waiting to hear again from McCabe."

McCabe, McCoy. Donaldson's friends all seemed Irish. He called McCabe "John." He called McCoy "Mac." If he thought of them as belonging to different species, he didn't admit it to himself.

Others were arriving. There were four TA mechanics and a maintenance foremen. The other inspectors were men who knew airplanes, with police and aviation backgrounds, and a couple of explosive experts.

Directing the search was the Chief Inspector for Airport Security. Here's what they had to inspect:

The 747 has been called "Queen Mary of the air." It also has been called "Holiday Inn with wings." Even as she ages (more than 20 years in service), the 747 remains King of the jumbo jets with little threat for sheer size from future planned transports.

Facts: The Wright brothers' historic first flight was shorter than the length of a 747. The entire flight might have been conducted in the cabin. Place a 747 on a football field from nose to tail and it would cover 75 yards. The wings would overhang the sidelines. The tail rises six and a half stories high.

The double-decked nose suggests a whale, distinguishing the 747 from other jets. Its mammoth appetite for fuel calls for two tank cars to serve it more than 47,000 gallons (316,000 pounds of fuel, enough to keep a family car running for 60 years: the equivalent of a swimming pool on each wing.

Paint markings—cosmetics— add 500 pounds to her 800,000 pounds gross weight. When hostessing for over 400 guests aloft, haute cuisine service in first class (less haute in economy) uses 491 coffee cups, 972 plates, 847 glasses, 176 bottles of wine and 25 gallons of liquor/liqueurs.

Thrust from one of her four engines provides more power than all three engines on her baby sibling 727. A failed engine fails to alarm her. Even if two engines fail, she can manage a safe landing. Throughout the plane there is redundancy: two pilots, three navigation systems, two or more of everything.

A sufficiently large hole in the fuselage will foil Boeing's best efforts. At best a passenger or two may be sucked through the hole. At worst, the plane goes down. It depends on the hole, where it is, other things. The pilot and his experience may be irrelevant. On the other hand, the pilot, with heroics and luck, might bring the business to a happy conclusion. The choppy Atlantic isn't very inviting.

The inspectors knew this. They had a lot to inspect in three hours.

They began. The chief inspector had a checklist and schematic diagram of the airplane. The men scattered out, checking overhead racks, foldout trays, seats, lavatories. Outside, the cargo compartments were opened and searched. Sniff dogs prowled through the cabins, cockpit, cargo compartments. Placed throughout the plane were dozens of inspection panels, almost invisible to the casual observer. Like the rest of the plane, most are dural: an aluminum alloy. Inspectors haven't time to unscrew or unsnap each panel and look behind. To McCoy and Donaldson, their choice of panels to inspect seemed as random as the placement of the panels by Boeing in Seattle eight years earlier.

To McCoy, too random. Climbing aboard the plane, he produced his own Phillips screwdriver from his jacket pocket. He began unscrewing panels the inspectors missed. Behind him were tubes, cables, plumbing, electrical circuits—or empty space.

Back on the ground McCoy scrutinized the long trailing edge of the wings, flaps down, his flashlight exposing the innards.

"They're skipping the APU," McCoy said.

"It's pretty inaccessible," Donaldson said.

"Not to a phony mechanic who knows his way around."

McCoy waved to a man in brown coveralls. "Hey, listen, get a cherrypicker out here. I want to look at that."

The man looked at McCoy, shrugged, walked away. Donaldson looked up at the APU—initials for Auxiliary Power Unit.

A 747 has four engines on the wing and a fifth engine concealed in the tail. Most people do not know the fifth engine exists, a DC-9 jet engine built in the tail structure, completely enclosed. On the ground it provides power for lights, hydraulics, air conditioning and heat.

By the time the cherrypicker had hoisted McCoy to the level of the APU, he was a small figure in blue with a pilot's cap and coat flapping in the wind. He began opening panels with his screwdriver.

Donaldson thought this was a little dumb, but respected McCoy too much to say anything. The man has super technical knowledge and could fix anything. Watching him work four stories above the ground, Donaldson thought about their long friendship.

Mac was 57. Former Air Force mechanic/crew chief. Donaldson knew Mac's resume by heart. He knew why Mac had chosen TA flights to Germany: to renew visits with a family he had known in the Air Force. Donaldson knew about McCoy's seriously ill wife. He knew McCoy would like to retire, but couldn't see his way clear.

The man who had brought the cherrypicker came up to Donaldson with a portable telephone. He handed the phone to Donaldson.

"New York," he said.

McCabe's husky voice cut through the static. "Ron. Where are you now?"

"Watching them go over the plane. How are you doing, John?"

"High and mighty."

"That's for damned sure." Donaldson could never quite believe that his old Vietnam buddy was now his boss.

"How do you read it?" McCabe asked.

"Not much to read. A man calls, says there will be a bomb, watch for plastic. I like that. Watch for plastic. We're watching."

"Be a little tough for the average guy to get hold of plastic. Now a terrorist . . . "

"What's the chance of a terrorist?" Donaldson asked.

"Interpol is looking into a couple of Libyans. Last seen in Frankfurt. No luck so far."

"Any passengers look suspicious?"

"The names were faxed to passport services in Washington and J. Edgar Hoover. They're checking. Not much time. Know where the other passengers are from?"

"I can guess."

"Sixteen countries. Zambia, Saudi Arabia, East Germany, the map of Europe. No way to check most of them, though Interpol is trying. You can knock the U.S., but we can still run more people faster through a computer than anyone else, certainly the third worlders. Know what we'll find?"

"Sure," Donaldson said. "The Americans. You can throw out 75 percent as business men on travel, families on vacation, children, some military on emergency leave, ladies over 90."

"You're off three percentage points," McCabe said. "Losing your touch."

"Okay," Donaldson went on. "The others will get more attention. Ten percent will be doubtful. Hippies, activists, maybe a rapist or a man with a missing wife. You'll narrow it down to four people."

"Three," McCabe said. "No rapist, but there was a guy with a missing wife. Another did a sit-in outside the White House. The third married to a Palestinian."

"Not much there."

"Not much."

There was silence and then McCabe said: "You know what is crazy?"

"Yeah. I know."

"One passenger. One out of one-seventy-seven. One passenger in a plane that carries four-hundred plus. How do you figure it?"

"I can't," Donaldson said. "There can't be that many chickens."

"We're trying to reach some of them. Everybody seems to have checked out of their hotels. Running names against other flights going to the U.S. Bound to find some."

"Know anything about the passenger who's going?"

"Not much. FBI draws blank. Been overseas once. London, 1987. From Omaha."

"The only one with guts," Donaldson said.

"Maybe. Maybe he knows something or doesn't know something. Security is talking to him now in the departure lounge. There will be an FBI agent aboard."

"So it'll seem like two passengers?"

"No. I think we'll have him dress like a Captain or a co-pilot, depending on whose coat we can find. Deadheading to the U.S. If our only passenger has any ideas—God help us—he might be less careful around a deadheading pilot. Dumb clucks, everybody knows.

"Sounds like we're flying."

"Sure, if you don't find a bomb. Or do and remove it. Either way. 'Course, it's your decision."

Right, my decision, Donaldson thought. McCabe, the high and mighty. But the book said they've made the decision together, and Donaldson, this time, agreed with McCabe. Fly.

"Talk to you later," McCabe said. Donaldson looked at the plane, the gray sky, McCoy descending on the orange cherrypicker. He decided to see how things were going in Freight.

The sign over the wide double doors said Flugfracht. There were about 10,000 pounds of air freight to inspect. What was the chance of finding a half pound of plastic—if that's what it was—taped to the underside of a wooden slat?

Dogtime. They supposedly could smell plastic from six feet away. Seven dogs, freight spread over a half acre. The dogs wandered around, three on leashes, four loose. They walked between stacked-up containers well above their heads. They sniffed. Amid the spare parts from Mercedes in Stuttgart there was a small tractor, some Grundig TV sets, a refrigerator, tagged and boxed.

They sniffed. If ever German shepherds, with their amazing noses, can ever look bored, these looked bored.

The dozen humans, Germans but not shepherds, in brown coveralls, herded about by an assistant chief inspector in a worsted business suit, showed little more interest than the dogs. If there was any design behind why they passed up a dozen crates to focus attention on the next—to haul it out and push it through an acromegalic X-ray machine—it was not evident.

At least it was not evident to Donaldson. The book said, "Everything must be X-rayed, opened or left." Most, this time around, was left. How could it be otherwise? A dozen men, two or three hours. Seven dogs.

Donaldson liked dogs. He owned dogs. But he could not believe that dogs could smell a molecule or two of some inert material six feet from its source.

He shrugged it off. He had never thought of flying as anything but risky, despite the talk about it being safer than any other way of getting people from A to B.

He turned around and saw Harvey "Bud" Fowler Jr. Coming in the door.

"Over here, Bud," he said, loudly but unnecessarily. Bud had seen him at once.

"Well, Captain," Bud drawled, reminding Donaldson of a movie pilot drawling. Bud was nothing if not typecast.

He was also a drunk. Like the German shepherds, Donaldson sniffed. It was automatic, dating back to Fowler's pilot treatment program when Donaldson was given the responsibility for monitoring his sobriety.

He could remember smelling Fowler's breath. In fact, he had turned Fowler in to professional standards two years before, although Fowler was not supposed to know this. He had smelled his breath in the cockpit— Jesus Christ, in a cockpit—of a 747 flying from Athens to Chicago.

Over the years, Donaldson had known pilots who drank too much. Younger, in the military, he may have drank too much. But never before flying (well, once or twice, in Vietnam). And times had changed. ALPA—the Air Line Pilots Association—had a program. Admit you had a problem. Take the 30-day "Minneapolis plan" cure. Attend AA. Go to aftercare. Stay 100 percent dry. You would be watched for two years. They might call your wife or neighbors. People like Donaldson—your own Captain—would monitor you. Sniff. Look for the slightest hint: puffiness. Splotchy complexion. Eyelids at half mast. A tendency to doze off. A growling stomach.

Donaldson approved of the ALPA program. Drunks shouldn't fly. As far as he knew, Fowler hadn't touched the stuff for a year.

He still wished he had another co-pilot.

"Wish you had another co-pilot?" Fowler asked. Donaldson was startled. Could the man read his mind? Did he know . . .

"I know, Fowler said. "Should have been here sooner. Got tied up in duty free."

"Donaldson tried to smile. "Never too late. Be another couple of hours, assuming they don't find anything."

"They won't," Bud said. "Never do."

"Well, they have to look."

Bud walked over and patted a dog. Slender, handsome, in his white shirt and epaulets (three stripes). Donaldson wondered where his coat was. The book said you wore the coat when you were out and about.

Donaldson disliked Fowler. Fowler, he knew, disliked him even more. There were recent reasons and long ago reasons.

Donaldson wished he had another co-pilot.

Back on the tarmac, grumpy, arms akimbo, looking up at the Whale, Donaldson got another international phone call from McCabe.

"What's happening?" McCabe asked.

"Not much. Still looking."

"How much longer?"

"Another hour or so, I guess. Anything at your end?"

"Zero." McCabe paused and added, "Guy's wife showed up."

"Who?"

"Guy who had the wife missing."

"Oh, well scratch him, I guess," Donaldson said.

"He didn't check in anyway."

"Bombers aren't supposed to check in, are they?"

"Some do."

"The looney-tuners," Donaldson said.

"They're all looney-tuney. Some just don't want to die."

Silence. Then McCabe: "Ever think about 'Nam?"

"Sure. Now and then. You?"

"Sure. Never thought I'd wind up behind a desk."

"You're a lucky bastard, John."

"Bull . . . " McCabe remembered he was on a five-way transatlantic hookup.

"You were lucky in 'Nam," Donaldson said.

"You can say that again."

"Once more and you'd been an ace."

"Four were plenty. They aimed for your ass."

"I took pictures. No glory." Donaldson's favorite complaint.

"No SAMs," said his New York boss.

"Sure, there were SAMs. The difference was you could bomb and kill. I took pictures."

"Knock it off, Ron, you're supposed to be finding a bomb."

Donaldson said, "Know why I'm really ticked off?"

"Guess I'll find out," McCabe said, thinking of the five-way party line.

"Because I'm ahead of you in seniority and you're the big cheese. Life's unfair."

"Know your real problem?" McCabe said.

"Just killing time."

"Bored, you mean. What they say about flying? Ninety-nine percent boredom, one percent panic."

Donaldson was tired of McCabe and cliches.

"Looks like they're winding up," he said. "If there's a bomb, they didn't find it."

"There was never a bomb."

"Easy talk from a ground-pounder," Donaldson said, knowing

McCabe hated the word. But he agreed with McCabe. Another nut. Another waste of time.

He and Susan would be having a very late dinner in D.C.

Luggage security begins at the check-in counter. Corrigan had placed his brown leather bag on the scales beside the counter. He was asked to unlock it. The bag was tagged and put on the conveyor belt. It moved quickly away to the baggage room on the lower level. A security man went through the luggage while a dog walked around it, nose quivering. The luggage was then placed back on the conveyor belt and passed through the metal detector.

If all goes well, as it did in Corrigan's case, the bag is placed on a baggage cart linked to three or four other carts, pulled by a little diesel tractor. The carts ordinarily carry 500 or 600 bags. Ordinarily they are placed in large metal or canvas containers. In airport jargon this is called containerization.

This was not ordinary. For this extraordinary trip, rows of empty containers would have looked silly.

Almost as silly as a single bag on a 60-foot cart train chugging out to a remote 747.

A single piece of luggage, escorted across the tarmac to the yawning cargo compartment in the belly of a giant humpbacked flying machine.

A single piece of luggage for the flying machine's only passenger.

5

Takeoff

The Boeing engineers sat around a table looking like they had just watched their wives deliver quadruplets.

On the table was a mockup of the first 747.

"You could play a full-court basketball game on one wing," boasted an engineer who had been a ninth round draft choice in the NBA eight years before.

"Hey," somebody said. "Where does the pilot sit?"

"The pilot?"

"Yeah. Can't fly a plane without a pilot."

"You sure? With all those computers?"

"Positive."

The engineers looked at the mockup, and one said, "But where?"

"Up here," one said, poking a finger at the nose.

"But that's the upper lounge. We'll lose passenger seats."

"Only a few. There's just three in the cockpit . . . airlines won't let fat guys fly."

Total sacrifice: six seats.

That's how the world's largest jetliner got a cockpit the size of a walk-in closet.

❧

Donaldson didn't mind the walk-in closet. He could reach everything, cuff the co-pilot on the ear if necessary. It had never been necessary, but on this flight . . . his gloom deepened.

The co-pilot slid into his seat. McCoy sat behind him. He had a swivel seat so he could face his engineer's panel or swing around and face forward. Behind the captain were two seats for the occasional flight inspector or deadheading pilot who dropped in to visit.

In the past, the captain would occasionally see a friend or neighbor on the flight and ask if he would like to sit in the cockpit and watch the take-off. From his observer's seat, the friend would witness something that would remain with him all his life: his old buddy, an ordinary guy who liked to barbecue hamburgers in the backyard, not particularly muscular, pull back the yoke in his short-sleeved shirt and lift an 800,000-pound, football field-sized aircraft off the ground and into the insubstantial air.

It seemed a miracle. Not many got an invitation to witness it anymore, in the age of bombers, terrorists and highjackers. Who knows a friend or neighbor so well to say he couldn't possibly be one of the above.

Behind the cockpit was the upper lounge for business class. Below was first class. Passengers in the forward three rows were in front of the cockpit, a half dozen well-heeled passengers plunging first into the oxygen-starved air.

Behind first was more business, the rest coach.

The single passenger sat in section D, one section from the rear of the aircraft. He stored his carryon in the overhead bin, took an aisle seat, and sat his cowboy hat in the seat next to him.

The purser, friendly skies written all over him, had suggested that he sit in first class, but he shook his head and walked back to section D. Maybe he liked to fold down the armrests between seats and take a nap, something he couldn't do in business or first.

The FBI agent disguised as a co-pilot sat in first class, some fifty yards forward. The flight attendants walked up and down the aisles, feeling foolish.

Everybody on the plane felt a little foolish. A little nervous. Both.

Except for the only passenger who sat in coach, hands folded, a picture of contentment.

They offered him a magazine and he said No, thank you.

They didn't offer him a drink because it was coach and they were still on the ground.

The FBI guy wondered if he should change seats, sit next to the passenger. His cover would be blown instantly. He stayed put, for the moment.

❦

The inspectors were still aboard looking for a bomb when the eleven

33

attendants arrived in a Volkswagen van. There was no jetway so they climbed the steps, women in high heels, to L-1 door, the forward passenger door on the left side of the plane. They deposited their bags in overhead bins and fanned out through the plane. Susan Donaldson climbed the spiral stairs to the upper deck where she would serve the lounge and cockpit. The purser with his thinning hair and rosy cheeks was smiling his friendly skies smile, but seemed unsure what to do.

One attendant named Lois Lister walked through L-1 and slumped into the closest seat to the open door. To her right was the forward galley and in front, across from the entryway, was a stub bulkhead with a white telephone in a niche.

For the next 40 minutes, while the inspectors finished inspecting, she looked at the bulkhead and its telephone. As the last inspector passed in front of her and out the door, she could be certain of one thing:

In the forty minutes she had sat there, the panel under the telephone on the bulkhead had not been touched. The inspectors worked from rear to front. There was a pretty good chance it had not been inspected before she got on the plane.

They couldn't, of course, inspect every panel on the plane. The ground delay would be intolerable.

If anyone was paying attention to Lois Lister—nobody was—they might have noticed a suggestion of amusement around the corners of her mouth as the cabin door slammed shut.

Donaldson was strapped in his seat, waiting for the "cabin secure" call from the purser. He settled back for a routine westbound return to the States. Having gone through eighty-four items on the preflight checklist and finding no problems, his mind resorted to trivia and reverie.

Westbound flights had odd numbers, like 131; eastbound even numbers. Millard Fillmore was the 13th President. Dover was the capitol of Delaware. He tried to remember who had won the last five Super Bowls. All he could think of was 49ers. He remembered scenes from his honeymoon.

Ways to make the time pass. Ways, on this trip, to shake off the uneasiness. Months of tedium, then stark terror: a pilot's life, as McCabe had said.

Cabin secure. Engine start normal. Taxi out uneventful. Donaldson pulled into takeoff position on runway seven left. When the control tower said "cleared for takeoff," his thoughts focused instantly on business.

McCoy adjusted his seat closer to the throttle quadrant between the two pilots seats, ready to trim the thrust—align each engine's power— once takeoff began. Donaldson released the brakes and slowly advanced the throttles.

The co-pilot called out V-1 (V for velocity) when the speed reached 125 knots. At this speed, the pilot still had time to abort the takeoff. When the speed reached 158 knots, the co-pilot called out "V-R" (R for rotate), meaning it was too late to abort and telling Donaldson to pull back on the control wheel and lift, or rotate, the nose upward.

Slowly, the big plane responded. Donaldson scanned his instruments: airspeed, rate of climb, radio altimeter. He remembered his first takeoff in a DC-3 at 90 miles per hour, compared to 200 miles per hour in the 747. The DC-3 only cruised at 180 miles per hour. Donaldson loved both planes equally.

Takeoff is serious; no time for small talk. The cockpit voice recorder is a constant snitch to the accident investigators assigning "probable caus-es" to pilot error. The only conversation allowed is a tightly scripted command and response. Sometimes the script was tighter than others, but Donaldson ran it by the books on this one.

"Up gear," he said.

Bud Fowler Jr. pulled up on the landing gear lever. Green lights flick-ered, then a red light came on. The nose wheel doors opened to receive the nose gear accompanied by sounds of rushing air, whirring hydraulic motors, metallic clanks, all heard in the cabin below. For white-knuckled aerophobics, it was not a comforting sound. Bud responded, "Gear's up," and returned the gear lever to neutral. The sounds ended and the plane flew faster and labored less.

"Flaps five," Donaldson said. Bud moved the flap lever to the five degree position and said, "Flaps five." No accident investigation would fault them.

The plane continued to pick up speed as Donaldson called out, "Climb thrust." McCoy, crouching forward and clutching the throttles, slowly retarded all four back to the climb power settings, noting reduced fuel flows and exhaust gas temperatures. All the while, he scanned his massive instrument panel monitoring electrical and hydraulic systems, cabin pressure and temperature, and some three hundred dials, gauges, switches and lights.

The 800,000-pound plane had been literally sucked into the air. Speed alone wouldn't do it. There was too much drag and gravity. Wind rushing under the flat surface of the wing produced a positive pressure pushing up. Because the top surface of the wing was curved, wind shot over the surface, creating a vacuum, or negative pressure.

Drag and gravity were defeated when the thrust produced enough positive pressure under the wing and negative pressure over the wing to lift the plane. The computer knew exactly when this would happen. It had been fed the airport altitude (Frankfurt was 400 feet above sea level), wind, temperature and load.

As always, the computer was right. One-thirty-one lifted off at 16:32 hours, two hours and forty-two minutes late.

Next: retract the wing flaps and relax for the balance of the flight. Before Donaldson could say "flaps up," the cockpit call bell rang. His jaw clamped tight. Calls to the cockpit during takeoff were never made except in emergencies.

Freda Van Valkenburgh was sitting in a front row seat in section E. She could see the passenger sitting forward and to her right in section D.

Freda was from a small town in Ohio, had modeled for a time in New York, then attended TA's Flight Attendant Academy in Chicago. This was her third flight.

As the plane lifted from the ground she saw the passenger stand up and remove his bag from the overhead bin. He stood by his seat and opened it. He removed a small gun-metal gray box from the bag.

Freda froze for a moment, then shouted, "Sit down! The seat belt sign is still on. You must sit down!"

He didn't sit down. He rummaged some more in his bag.

Freda lunged from her seat. She plucked the phone from the stub bulkhead in front of her. She called the cockpit.

Ordinarily she would have known better, but this was no ordinary flight.

The "plus three, minus eight" rule on TA was sacred. It means the cockpit was not to be bothered on takeoffs plus three minutes and for expected landing time minus eight minutes except in emergencies.

But here it was. Someone on the interphone from downstairs. Donaldson acknowledged the call with a disgusted, "What the hell?" Mac, see what they want."

Mac removed the handset from its holder between the pilots and spoke into the mouthpiece. "Cockpit."

"Mac, this is Freda, Freda Van Valkenburgh. Section E. Our passenger is standing up and the seatbelt sign is still on."

"I know it's still on. Tell him to sit down. Ask what he's looking for. Keep an eye on him. Skipper may send the FBI man back to check him out."

Mac relayed the conversation to Donaldson, who was concentrating on the departure routing and altitude clearances. Frankfurt controllers were sticklers, unforgiving about any deviations on departures. Noise abatement violations were viewed as seriously as traffic foul-ups.

Donaldson made a decision. "Tell her to leave him alone. Don't bother the FBI man. First things first.

"Up flaps."

The co-pilot turned off the seatbelt sign at 20,000 feet. Usually the captain remained in the cockpit at least until they reached 31,000 feet, where they would fly for an hour to burn off enough fuel to get to 35,000 feet, the cruising altitude for oceanic crossings. (Civilian planes flew at odd-thousand feet, the military even-thousand, except for the Russians, who flew at any altitude. On certain flights one always had to look out for the Russians.)

Usually only an urgent call from nature—turistas they call it, but it was more likely sauerbraten—would persuade the captain to leave the cockpit before reaching cruise altitude. Today, however, he had his mind on the passenger in section D.

It wasn't so unusual for a passenger to ignore the seatbelt sign and stand up during takeoff, and even bolt for the laboratory, perhaps a victim of sauerbraten himself.

But this was not a usual passenger. He was the only passenger, and he had violated the rules. Donaldson wanted to talk to him.

The passenger was listening to a Sony Walkman. The captain sat across the aisle and motioned for him to take off the earphones.

"Enjoying the flight?"

"Sure."

"Certainly got the plane to yourself."

The passenger lifted his eyebrows and made a deprecatory gesture with his hands, as if to say, "Don't blame me."

Donaldson hadn't smoked in 15 years, but at that moment, if someone had offered him a cigarette, he probably would have taken it. Except it was a non-smoking zone.

"See you brought your own music." Donaldson glanced at the earphones the airline provided, sealed and sanitized in cellophane. The man didn't answer.

"What you listening to?"

The man held up a plastic cassette holder. The cover said "The All-Time Greatest Hits of Roy Orbison."

"My idol," said the passenger. He seemed serious.

"Didn't he die some time ago?"

"December 6, 1988."

"Oh," Donaldson said. He wasn't much of a music fan. "Country Western?"

"Absolutely not," the passenger said. "Ballads, rockabilly. Pure genius. Elvis Presley said he was the best singer in the world. Elvis was right."

"How old was he when he died?"

"Fifty-two." Heart attack. He had a triple by-pass nine years before."

"You seem to know a lot about him."

"When you read a rock 'n roll reference book, all they say is 'Sad songs, big voice, dark glasses.' They leave out his tragic life."

"Tragic?"

"His wife was killed in a motorcycle accident with Roy riding just ahead of her when it happened."

"That must have been tough."

"Two years later, a fire destroyed his house in Hendersonville, Tennessee, killing two of his three children. From that point on, he refused to attend funerals."

Donaldson shared with the passenger a moment of silence, then asked, "Orbison re-marry?"

"Yes. In 1969, he married a young German woman named Barbara Wellhoven. That's why I came to Germany. To be with her."

❦

Abruptly, Corrigan changed the subject. "Why so few passengers?" he asked.

"That's what we're wondering. Why just you?"

"But if everybody had showed up, you would still be less than half full. June should be a busy month."

"Usually is." Donaldson deliberated for a moment about whether to say more. "Maybe you read about a guy buying up Transatlantic stock about a year ago. They called it a leveraged takeover. Junk bonds."

"Right. I read about it. Tarkington, wasn't it? Made millions on leveraged buyouts. Corporate raider. Eccentric. A recluse."

"Add crazy. He's done some crazy things since he became CEO."

Corrigan looked thoughtful. With the edge of his hand, he deepened the crease in his cowboy hat.

For the first time, Donaldson showed some emotion. "First, he does away with the frequent flyer plan. Retroactively! Thousands of people had earned free tickets and upgrades to first class, which he wouldn't honor. Got the company a bad press, not to mention a bunch of lawsuits."

Donaldson looked glum. "People liked the frequent flyer bonuses. All the lines have them. That's one reason passengers have been deserting us."

He stopped looking glum and continued, "Another reason. Everybody raised their fares in May, anticipating full flights, and then lowered them again when passengers rebelled and stayed home. But not Tarkington. He kept the high fares. He even did away with discount fares! More desertions."

"Sounds like he wants the airline to go under."

"It's possible. We've seen it in other companies. Go chapter eleven, sell out, take a tax write-off, or reorganize. Reorganizing means lower salaries. The unions are furious."

"He might be pleased if your plane was bombed. The last straw."

"Maybe old Tark is the bomber. If there was a bomb, which there isn't."

"Tarkington that nutty?"

"Who knows? Mysterious guy. No interviews, no pictures—hides out in a Vegas hotel. Hasn't been seen in public in five years."

"Like Howard Hughes."

"Different hotel. Wonder if he has phobias?"

6

Washington and Omaha

Stephen Geopolis was halfway across the Arlington Memorial Bridge when he got the call. It was Friday morning. The phone in the Cutlass Supreme tingalinged and he said, "Geopolis."

"Ferris here." Geopolis looked at his watch: 8:05. Ferris was in early.

"Tried your home. Already left. Why so early?"

"Today's the day we nail Garcia. I hope."

"Not today," Ferris said. "You've been switched."

"Switched? Why the hell switched? I've been working for months on this case. Today's the day. Maybe."

"Sorry, Steve. Wasn't my decision. Fergis says to put you on the bomb case."

"What bomb case?"

Bomb threat in Frankfurt. Everyone's taking it seriously."

Geopolis drove behind the Lincoln Memorial and headed north on 23rd Street. He had left Alexandria 20 minutes before. Traffic on the parkway had been heavy. He wished he had been up earlier, had at least a cup of coffee. Helen would sleep until nine.

But he had been too happy about the Garcia case, too eager. Now his happiness evaporated and he was mad. He took it out on Ferris.

"God damn it, not fair. Another idiotic bomb threat. Anybody can handle that shit."

"Talk to Fergie. Anyway you're on it. Thought you should know. Give you a few minutes to cool off." Ferris went off the line.

Geopolis took Constitution Avenue past The Ellipse and turned north on 14th. The mansard roof and bullseye windows of the restored Willard gleamed in the morning light.

He turned right on F Street and another right three blocks east. Passing

Ford's Theater, he swung into the underground garage of the J. Edgar Hoover Building, showing his I.D. to the guard. Already a line of tourists had formed around the building, waiting for the day's first guided tour.

He took the elevator to the fourth floor and walked down a corridor of what was widely believed to be the ugliest building in Washington. He said good morning to Jane in the reception area and walked into his office. The office was plain with a signed picture of the director on the wall and government-issue furniture and carpet. There was a couch and sitting on it was Ferris, red hair flaming in the light from the window facing Pennsylvania Avenue. You could see the Justice Department across the street and today, as on many mornings, Geopolis pictured the late John Mitchell on the balcony smoking his pipe while Vietnam protesters demonstrated with placards and police with truncheons waited behind barricades, deciding whom to pounce on next. Geopolis had snapped pictures from another window—Hoover's monument hadn't been built yet—and these pictures were now in a vault somewhere, blackmail fodder for the country's next McCarthy.

Geopolis collapsed in a chair near the couch and ran his fingers through his thick gray hair.

"Okay, George. Let's have it."

"Still sore?"

"Sure, but what can I do? Ferguson is boss. Five more years and I retire and go fishing."

"You don't fish."

"I'll learn. Maybe I'll practice law."

Ferris handed him a file. It had one sheet in it. Geopolis scanned it.

"Why are they taking this seriously?"

"Brevity. Specificity. No bullshit."

"He specified plastic, so that makes it specific?"

"That's how Interpol sees it."

"What's the airline think?"

"Don't know. Waiting for you to get here."

There was a phone on the coffee table. Geopolis picked it up. "Jane, I'm dying. Can you get me a sweet roll and a cuppa black." He looked at Ferris. "Want anything?"

"Not now. There's a hookup between Frankfurt and New York. We'd better join it."

There wasn't much to say. Interpol was faxing the passenger list to Washington. One hundred and seventy-seven names was a piece of cake for passport and the FBI computers. The plane for TA 131 couldn't be searched until it arrived in Frankfurt tomorrow morning, Saturday.

Still Geopolis had to be available, wait for information to come in. The FBI computer might provide some suspects. As agent in charge, he would be responsible for deciding how suspicious were the suspects.

It was mid-morning, Friday. The passenger list was supposedly on the way.

Friday, 16:00. Three suspects.

The Special Agent in Houston was talking to the mother of a man whose wife had disappeared. The man was on a business trip to Bern. The mother didn't think he was very concerned about the wife. The wife's psychiatrist said she had a bad case of erotomania—love affairs with fantasy lovers. Her current letch was for Robert Redford. The mother thought she might have flown to Hollywood. A snapshot was shown to ticket agents at the two Houston airports. Except for the erotomania, she was pretty normal: good wife and mother. Her husband was selling carburetors to the Swiss. Good job history.

The man with the Palestinian wife was enroute to Frankfurt, accompanied by the wife. They would be met at the airport by Interpol.

A Berkeley astrophysicist, concerned about saving the whale, had set cross-legged on the sidewalk outside the north fence of the White House for 24 hours—18 years ago. Since then, nothing. He was attending a peace conference in Geneva. He was flying Swiss Air to Frankfurt on Saturday morning and would be met by Interpol at the airport.

Geopolis slept on his office couch Friday night, trying to digest a pizza the size of a manhole cover. The phone rang from time to time. By 4:00 Washington time—10:00 in Frankfurt—the wife had come home, having spent 36 consecutive hours in a local Days Inn watching Redford movies on the VCR. The Palestinian wife turned out to be Jewish immigrant from Brooklyn and the astrophysicist announced he had changed flights and would be taking Pan Am. He had read about the bomb threat.

The man with the Jewish wife had decided to lay over in Frankfurt for a day, to see the sights. The Houston man hadn't shown up at the airport, but his mother said he had called home and was glad his wife had returned.

At 7:00 the day of the flight McCabe was on the phone. "Strangest thing, Mr. Geopolis."

"Wha? Said the half-asleep agent.

"An hour before one-thirty-one was supposed to fly and only one passenger has shown up."

"One passenger?"

"A doctor from Omaha."

Geopolis sipped some cold coffee from a plastic mug. "What do you make of it?"

"It's very puzzling," McCabe said. "Ever since Northwest started warning passengers about threats, people have changed flights, but never this many."

"Have you talked to any of them?"

"Some. They all say it's too dangerous."

The agent yawned and sat up. He switched on a lamp. "Well, what's his name?"

"Who's name?"

"The only passenger."

"Going to check him out? He's the only one with guts to fly."

"Got his address in Omaha?"

"Sure. Wait a minute. Two-four-zero-one-zero Mountain Ridge Road."

"Think I'll call Omaha."

He waited until eight o'clock—seven Omaha time—to place the call. Nobody was home. For the next three hours he called every fifteen minutes. Saturday morning and nobody home. Have they left for the weekend?

TA 131 was crossing the English Channel when Geopolis finally reached Mrs. Robert Corrigan in Omaha. Someone—a teenager?—had finally answered the phone and said she could be reached at the Omaha Country Club. She answered the poolside phone at 10:03 her time.

"Yes?"

"Mrs. Corrigan? Robert Corrigan's wife?"

"Yes."

"I'm calling about your husband. My name is Stephen Geopolis. I am with the Federal Bureau of Investigation in Washington."

"Have you found him?"

"What do you mean 'found him?' Is he missing?"

"Of course. Isn't that why you've called?"

Geopolis took a deep breath. "Mrs. Corrigan, we didn't know your husband was missing. How long has he been missing?"

"Five days. The Omaha Police . . . the Missing Persons people . . . have been looking. We've been terribly worried."

She didn't sound worried, but then it had been five days.

"Well, Mrs. Corrigan, we weren't exactly looking for your husband, but we did find him."

"Wonderful! Is he alright?"

"As far as we know. Right now he's on an airplane flying to America. He's the only passenger on the airplane. That's why I called."

"The only passenger? Isn't that . . . strange?"

"That's what we think. Tell me, Mrs. Corrigan. Tell me about your husband's disappearance."

Silence, then: "Well, you see, we don't know. Bob's not the type of man to disappear, ever. We've been very worried."

"He didn't leave a note? Call?"

"No, not a thing. He disappeared last Saturday. I thought he was at the hospital, but he wasn't. The nurse called me. He had patients to see and he wasn't there."

"Has this happened before?"

"Never!" Bob was the most dependable man in the world. Everyone counted on him. His patients, me, the children. We've all been tremendously upset." Pause. "You're certain he's alright? He had no reason for going away, not saying anything."

Geopolis was thinking, I'd better get to McCabe about this, right away. "Mrs. Corrigan," he said, "is there any reason your husband should leave home?"

"None. His patients think he's wonderful.. His children think he's wonderful. I . . ."

"You think he's wonderful?"

"Yes. Yes, I do. I think he's wonderful, too." Her voice cracked. Geopolis wondered if she was crying.

"Money problems?"

"None that I know of. He takes care of the money. He's never said anything. We live well."

"Health problems?"

"He may still be a little weak. He was in the hospital for nearly a month."

"As a patient?"

"Yes. I guess you don't know about that either."

"Tell me, Mrs. Corrigan." He was sure now that she was crying.

"My throat's dry. Let me get a Coke from the machine."

She was back a minute later. Her voice was faint. He could barely hear her.

"It was in all the papers. You didn't read about it?

"Maybe it wasn't in the Washington papers. You'll have to tell me."

"Bob had a partner. His name was George Donovan. George and Bob were in George's car in the hospital driveway. George had a gun. He shot Bob. Then he shot himself. In the chest. And he was a chest surgeon, like Bob."

"My God," Geopolis said. He really had to reach McCabe now. Let the pilot know. The plane was somewhere over the Atlantic.

"What happened to the partner? George?"

"He died. It was suicide."

"Why did he shoot your husband?"

"Nobody knows. Bob and George had been friends for years. Both from the same town. Fraternity brothers. Went to medical school together. Naturally, they ended up partners."

"And no problems between them?"

"None that Bob can think of."

"Why would the partner commit suicide? Any ideas?"

"The psychiatrist said he snapped."

"Psychiatrist?"

"Yes, afterwards Betty Donovan, the wife, saw a psychiatrist. She was so mystified by the whole thing. The psychiatrist said George must have snapped. He said sometimes people just snap."

This tended to confirm Geopolis' opinion of psychiatrists.

"Before this all happened," he said. "Had your husband been acting different in some way? Like he was worried about something?"

"Well, he had been away a lot."

"Any reason?"

"Oh, yes. His practice was very demanding. Sometimes he didn't get home until midnight or later. Emergencies, whatever."

"Out of town trips?"

"Bob was a delegate to the medical association. In the last several months, before the . . . accident . . ."

Geopolis waited.

"He spent some weekends in Lincoln. Committee work. The legislature was meeting. Between Lincoln and patients, I might not see him for several days at a time. I understood. Bob was that way. Very conscientious. Civic minded."

"Mrs. Corrigan, I'm going to have to get off the phone. Let me ask you maybe a painful question, but I have to ask."

"I understand."

"Do you think patients, medical meetings, explain Dr. Corrigan being away so much?"

"Do I think he was seeing someone? Some woman perhaps?" There was a note of sarcasm.

"Well, yes. Did you think that?"

"Mr. . . . I'm sorry, I forgot your name. Bob and I have been married seventeen years, have two wonderful children. He loves them and, I guess, me. That's why we couldn't understand him leaving, just dropping out of sight. It made no sense."

"In all those years, he was . . . faithful?"

"I was sure of it."

"*Was* sure?"

Now, a long pause. Her voice was even fainter. "While he was in the hospital I decided to pay the bills. There was an American Express bill with three charges that I'm sure were mistakes."

"What for?"

"Three nights at the Red Lion Inn."

"Same nights he was in Lincoln?"

"I don't know. I didn't check."

"Afraid to check?"

"Bob said they were a mistake. I believed him."

"Where's the Red Lion Inn?"

"Here in Omaha. It's our nicest hotel. That's why it must be a mistake."

"I don't understand."

"Bob would never stay at the Red Lion Inn. Why would he? He has a home just a mile away. And . . . "

"Yes?"

"Too many people know him. Too big a chance. He'd be recognized. He wouldn't . . . " She definitely was crying.

"Do those things?"

"No, not Bob. You don't know Bob. He would never do those things!"

Before Geopolis hung up, he got the name of the Omaha detective in charge of the assault-suicide incident. That had been the coroner's verdict.

7

One Hour Out

"Alpha, bravo, Juliet, delta," Donaldson said.

"Ron?"

"Hello, John."

Every plane has a Selcal code. TA 131's code was ABJD. Selcal means select a call. The TA dispatcher at Kennedy would select a call to any plane anywhere. He had arranged a three-way patch-in on VHF satellite radio between McCabe's exec office in Rockefeller Plaza, Interpol in Frankfurt and Donaldson over the Atlantic.

McCabe was doing the talking.

"Mr. Geopolis at the Hoover building just called me and I used the direct line to Kennedy. Three of us are on the phone. Hello, everyone."

There were some murmured hellos.

"Ron, you're one hour out. Feel any safer?"

One pilot talking to another. Interpol and the dispatcher probably wouldn't understand.

"Home free. The kitchen timer didn't go off."

The oldest detonating device in airplane bomb threat history is the kitchen timer. A kitchen timer is a simple spring-wound timer device. Nothing complicated or technical. No batteries. One turn and in one hour it unwinds. A little bell rings. Time to take the roast out—or time for a bomb to explode.

In the old days, when the flight dispatcher informed the pilot just off the ground that a bomb might be aboard—and every old-timer had it happen at least once—the pilot would wait in suspense, every few minutes checking his Rolex. After an hour passed, he grinned and considered the threat officially ended. No kitchen timer on this trip.

That was the old days—the days of the amateur bomber who had

49

bought a $100,000 life insurance policy on his wife from the airport vend-
ing machine, just before kissing her goodbye at the gate.

"No help," Donaldson said. "No self-respecting terrorist would use a
kitchen timer."

"Maybe a barometer," McCabe said. They both laughed.

"What was it?" Donaldson asked. "Rod Serling? A book or a TV
show?" Neither could remember, but it started in the '50s with fiction and
ended in farce.

In fiction a barometer had been attached to a bomb. Barometers, mea-
suring atmospheric pressure, also indicate altitude. (A barometer is an
altimeter and vice versa.) When the barometer needle indicated an altitude
of, say, 5,000 feet, it armed the bomb. When the plane descended and
reached 5,000 feet again, the bomb went off. In fiction.

For a time, barometers became the bomb threatener's favorite detonator. "When your plane reaches 5,000 feet," the caller would say, "a bomb
will go off." Until the fad passed, dispatchers took it seriously. They
would dispatch flights to Denver or Salt Lake City—any airport above
5,000 feet. It was a hell of a nuisance.

Of course, no bomb was ever found. Years later, pilots were still talking about it. As, now, were McCabe and Donaldson, old pilots, old
friends.

"Back to your present problem," McCabe said.

"There's a problem?"

"Probably not. But FBI has some intelligence about your passenger.
We're obligated to pass it on."

"Shoot."

"He's been missing from home for five days. FBI called his wife."

"Think it's important."

"No idea. But there's something else."

"Go on."

"A bizarre shooting incident. Two doctors outside a hospital. One doctor shoots the other and then himself. The shooter dies. The shootee lives
and is hospitalized. Just got out of the hospital. The shootee is your passenger."

Donaldson was silent for a moment, then said, "I'll talk to him again."

8

Moore

By the time Geopolis reached Mrs. Corrigan at the Omaha Country
Club, he had been on the case for 27 hours. Not much had happened.
Three suspects had been found: all checked out OK. He, along with everyone else, was surprised to learn that one passenger, of 177, had taken the
flight.

Looking back, Geopolis wished he had been more surprised. He
wished he had called Omaha as soon as he learned the news. Wished he
hadn't waited until 7:00, Omaha time, to avoid awaking the wife. When
no one answered he was sorry he hadn't pushed it—called the Omaha
Police—done something. It was 11:00 when he reached her. TA 131 had
been flying for half an hour.

He simply hadn't considered the single passenger a suspect. Why
should he? It was the law of probabilities. Enough bomb threats and some
day only one passenger would show up.

Geopolis really called because he had nothing else to do.

By the time he had heard Mrs. Corrigan's story and passed it on to
McCabe in New York, the plane was about an hour out.

When he tracked Francis Moore to his house in south Omaha, where
he was having lunch with his 81-year-old mother, it took less than seven
minutes.

Moore answered the phone. "Sure," he said, "I remember the case.
Everyone here remembers. It was only—what was it—six weeks ago?"

"Was it really assault-suicide?"

"That's what the coroner said."

"You investigated?"

"That's right. I was working that night."

51

"When was it?"

"It was Tuesday. First, second week in May. Look, why the interest?" Geopolis told him.

"That's really something. Wait a minute. Let me get on another phone. I'm talking in the kitchen."

When Moore came back his voice had lowered to a whisper—as if afraid he might be overheard.

"Look, my notes are at the station. Maybe I'd better drive down there."

"How far away?"

"Ten or fifteen minutes, depending on traffic."

Geopolis said, "How's your memory."

"Good. Especially for this."

"Tell me what you remember. I'm fighting a clock."

"Looking at my pocket calendar. It was Tuesday, May 8. A call came in about eight. Almost dark."

Geopolis was reminded of something irrelevant. Most murders occur on Saturday, fewest on Tuesdays. But the coroner's verdict did not include murder.

"It was Dr. Corrigan, calling 911 from a car phone. Asked for help. Said he had been shot by his partner. The partner shot himself, may be dead. Said he was in the driveway of Douglas County Hospital, to get there fast. I think that's all he said."

"Did he identify himself?"

"No. But a patrol car got there first and called us, said it was Dr. Corrigan and someone else. Parked about 20 feet from the emergency room. Convenient as hell if you've just been shot. By the time we got there Corrigan and his partner were in the ER. The partner was dead. Corrigan seemed in shock but conscious."

"Did you know Corrigan?" Geopolis had the impression that he did.

"Not personally. But I've seen him on TV. I know his reputation."

"What is his reputation."

"Outstanding. The Jaycees voted him the Omaha Man of the Year. He got a lot of publicity when NU started doing liver transplants."

"NU?"

"The University of Nebraska. The NU Medical Center is a few blocks north of county hospital. Corrigan got a lot of credit for the transplants, getting funding and so forth, but I don't think he did them. Bypasses were his thing."

"Was the partner as well known?"

"Not to me. Among doctors, perhaps. He and Corrigan were on the faculty of the medical center. Must have done pretty well. Since this happened, I saw their houses. Out by the country club. Ritzy."

"So," Geopolis said. "The partner dies, Corrigan lives. When did you hear what happened?"

"After the operation. They wheeled Corrigan right up to surgery. It was the next morning before I could talk to him."

"What did he tell you?"

"Crazy story. He and Donovan—Donovan was the partner—were sitting in the driveway, talking about patients. They did this several times a week, whenever they switched shifts. With no warning, Donovan pulls a pistol out of his pocket. He pokes it in Corrigan's stomach and pulls the trigger. The door opens somehow and Corrigan falls out onto the ground, shot in the belly."

Moore said, "Before going on, I'm closing the door. Be telling you things I haven't even told my mother."

He continued: "So here we have Corrigan lying on the ground outside the car and he hears a shot. He gets to his knees and looks in the car. Donovan is slumped over the steering wheel. Corrigan gets on the car phone and calls 911. That's it. That's all he could tell us."

"That's it?" Geopolis looked at his watch. They had been talking about 15 minutes. He'd better get the slow-talking Moore to speed up.

"Why did Donovan shoot Corrigan?"

"Corrigan hadn't the slightest idea. Friends for years. No friction between them, ever, if you can believe that. Even the wives were friends."

"Did you go into money, women?" Geopolis thought a minute. "Drugs?"

"Sure, all those things. Denies everything. Both partners making plenty of money. One bypass brings in thousands. Those guys are rich. Women? If so, no evidence. We've asked nurses, even patients. All you hear is how nice these guys were. Particularly Corrigan."

"Did you ask Mrs. Corrigan about another woman?"

"Yes. Nobody."

"Mrs. Donovan? Her husband?"

"Nobody."

So Geopolis now knew something Moore didn't. Not much but something.

❧

Moore wasn't finished. "I don't believe Corrigan," he said.

"You don't?"

"This is just between us. Corrigan is like a saint to people in this town."

"A hunch, new evidence, what?"

"Call it a hunch. That's why I've kept my trap shut. But listen to this." Geopolis listened.

"I talked with the surgeon. The surgeon told me Corrigan was amazingly lucky. The bullet passed through the lower colon and out the back. Missed the kidney. Missed the spinal cord. Missed important blood vessels. Even missed nerves you need to screw with."

"Why did he take a month to recover?"

"Peritonitis. A resistant infection. He could have died from the infection, but didn't."

"So he was lucky. Anything else?"

"There was nothing in his colon. No feces. It's a wonder he got peritonitis."

"When had he eaten last?"

"He says hours before. His last meal was breakfast."

"Does he usually miss lunch?"

"No, not usually."

"Anything else unusual?"

"I'm just quoting the surgeon here. When he opened the colon, he would have sworn the patient had recently had an enema."

❧

Francis Moore had been a pre-med at Creighton when a foreclosure of his father's farm west of Omaha catapulted him out of college and into the Omaha Police Department. He was 19. As a sophomore, he had been on the Creighton all-state wrestling team. A year later, he became the sole support for his widowed mother after his father crashed his pickup truck

54

into a bridge abutment.

A large, shaggy, slow-talking man, he had the longest seniority in the department, three years from retirement. He was a bachelor and lived with his mother in a bungalow in a middle-class neighborhood in south Omaha.

His interest in medicine, and disappointment about not becoming a doctor, had never abated. Some of his pre-med college friends practiced in Omaha and he occasionally had coffee with them.

"How do doctors usually kill themselves?" he asked Fred Bradshaw, internist, over a second cup. It was Wednesday, May 9, the morning after the assault-suicide.

"You're thinking about George Donovan," Bradshaw said, having read the morning paper. "You involved?"

Moore nodded and sipped his coffee.

Bradshaw sipped his. "Pills," he said. "When doctors commit suicide it's usually pills. I had a friend at the med school who asked a pharmacologist how much Elavil it would take to kill a person. 'How big a person?' he was asked. 'Oh, say about my size,' he said. The pharmacologist looked him over and said, 'Well, five or six grams ought to do it.' Two days later my friend died in the Holiday Inn out by Boys Town, overdosed on Elavil.

"Doctors," he went on, "have an inside track on pills. They know where to get them and how much to take. Or if they don't, they find out."

Moore, who read a little, said, "Hemingway's father was a doctor. He shot himself with a Smith and Wesson pistol."

"His son shot himself with a shotgun," said Bradshaw, who also read a little. "Some doctors know as much about guns as they do about pills. Was Donovan a gun lover?"

"Can't say. If a doctor does shoot himself, where is he most likely to shoot?"

Bradshaw pointed a finger in his mouth. "Soft palate. Every first year medical student knows that. You can't miss the brain stem."

"Donovan," Moore said, "shot himself in the chest. Does that tell you anything?"

"He pointed the barrel at his chest and pulled the trigger? That's an awkward thing to do. The wrist only bends about 90 degrees or less. Unless he held the gun with one hand and pulled the trigger with the other.”

“Possible. There were prints from only one hand.”

“Chest surgeon shoots himself in the chest,” Bradshaw reflected. “Probably knew where to aim.”

“The bullet enters his right ventricle. Died instantly.”

Bradshaw drank more coffee and munched on a piece of toast. “Took a hell of a chance.”

“How’s that?”

“Hell of a chance of surviving. It’s hard—or relatively hard—to shoot yourself in the chest and die. Most people who try it survive.”

“What’s the reason?”

“First, it’s hard to take aim. You have to hit the heart or one of the big vessels. Most of the chest is air. If you really had bad luck, you’d sever the spinal cord. You’d not only still be alive but paralyzed for life.”

“Wouldn’t a chest surgeon have a better chance of hitting the heart?”

“Not necessarily. Every doc knows where the heart is. Hearts aren’t really that large. They’re in constant motion, like plump eels. No, I think, of all people, a chest surgeon would appreciate how easy it is to miss the heart, particularly if you’re doing the shooting and it’s your heart.”

Moore was ruminating about Bradshaw’s views as he drove from the hotel coffee shop to the Corrigan home on Mountain Ridge Road.

“Mrs. Corrigan was wearing peach slacks and a charcoal sweater. Her dark hair was streaked with gray. Her tan was off to a good start.

“Lieutenant Moore,” he said. “Homicide.” He flipped open his badge case.

“Homicide?” She seemed startled. “Oh, yes, last night. That terrible business. Come in.”

She led him to a paneled family room with a 32-inch TV set and glass doors opening onto a patio. Beyond the patio was a swimming pool. It was 92 degrees outside and the air conditioning was on.

“I spent the night at the hospital,” she said. “They set up a cot, but I didn’t sleep. I couldn’t believe what happened.”

“I’ve talked with your husband. The doctor says he’ll be alright.”

“Thank God. He’ll be moved to the medical center today. The county hospital . . .”

She didn't finish. Moore knew she meant the county hospital wasn't good enough for her husband. Wards and poor people.

"Did your husband say what happened?"

"He was too weak to talk much, but I got the general picture."

"He says Dr. Donovan shot him and then himself."

She looked down at her hands. "Lieutenant Moore," she said, "that is the most utterly unbelievable thing I've ever heard."

"Tell me about your husband," Moore said.

She stretched, stifling a yawn, and said, "I'm sorry, I'm bushed. Later, can we?"

"Sure, I'll come back. Maybe a couple questions now."

"Okay."

"Any problems between your husband and his partner?"

"None that I know of."

"Money problems?"

"None that I know of."

"They were old friends, I hear."

"They grew up in a small town. Been with each other ever since."

"How long have you known your husband?"

"Since college. We met at a sorority dance."

"What kind of young man was he?"

"Look, I'm sorry. I've got to get some sleep."

"Anyone else I could talk to, someone who knows him well?"

She thought for a minute, eyelids drooping. "Try Jerry Herzog. Works at the Western Auto on Spruce. He grew up with Bob. Pals ever since."

That was the morning after the shooting. It would be more than six weeks before he would talk to Mrs. Corrigan again. When the time came, TA 131 would be flying across the Atlantic and Geopolis of the FBI would be pumping him for information.

Geopolis kept eyeing his watch. The plane was an hour out, somewhere over Scotland, and the slow-talking Moore was laying out his reasons for believing the Donovan-Moore thing was not what it seemed.

"One, the shot was a lucky shot. Miraculous, the doctor said. Two, Donovan was not suicidal, in my opinion."

"What's the basis for your opinion?"

"Okay, no note. Suicides usually leave notes or announce their intentions. No sign of depression. Corrigan didn't notice any signs, his wife didn't notice any signs."

"People hide it."

"Not that well. He was planning a trip with his family on the weekend. He asked his wife to get his clothes from the cleaners. Friends had been invited for dinner that very night."

"Was Donovan in debt?"

"Not according to his wife."

"Worried about his health?"

"Healthy as a horse."

"Had a mistress? Jilted?"

"Family man all the way. Spent every minute of his spare time with wife and kids. Little League. Took the kids fishing."

Geopolis was about to give up when Moore said, "One more thing. He had a half million dollar life insurance policy on himself."

"So, there's your motive. He wanted to set up his beloved family."

"The policy had a two-year suicide clause. If the insured died by suicide within the two-year period, the policy would be void. The widow didn't get a penny."

"Was the two years up?"

"Had 10 days to go."

"Point three," Moore said, "the bullet."

Geopolis looked at his watch.

Moore said, "Remember, I told you Corrigan fell out of the car after he'd been shot."

"Right."

"We found a little blood on the pavement next to the right hand door of the car. That made sense. When the ER people found Corrigan he was lying flat on his back outside the car."

"Go on. Can you hurry a little."

"When they lifted Corrigan onto a stretcher, there was a pinging sound. Like something metal had dropped on the pavement. Sure enough, they looked with a flashlight and there was a slug on the pavement. They assumed it was the slug that wounded Corrigan. They assumed it had

58

lodged in his back and fell out when they lifted him. And they assumed right.”

Geopolis’ impatience became almost unbearable. “Go on, man, get on with it.”

“The gun was lying on the car floor, under the steering wheel. Smith & Wesson, .32 caliber revolver, five shot. Two bullets had been fired. Ballistics checked the rifling. The slug that fell on the pavement was fired by the gun that shot Corrigan—and the gun that shot Donovan.”

“It all fits then. What’s the problem?”

“It may not be a problem. Folks I work with think I’m talking through my hat but I’m not so sure.”

“Go on. Quickly if you don’t mind.”

“Bullets for the gun come in short and long. These were short. Not much penetrating power. But the gun had been pushed right into Corrigan’s stomach. There were powder wounds on his abdomen. None on his clothes. He was wearing a jogging suit with a zippered jacket and the jacket was open.”

Geopolis was beginning to understand Moore’s problem but said nothing.

“Even a .32 short, shot at that range, would penetrate the abdominal wall, pass through the colon and come out the back. Not only come out but punch a hole in the seat. No hole.”

“And?”

“I have a theory. Before the bullet was fired, the slug had been removed. The power load had been reduced by removing some grains. A .32 short may not travel far, but it will penetrate the soft tissue we’re talking about—unless the powder load is reduced.”

Moore summed up. “Look at the problem. No suicide motive. No motive to shoot his partner. Chest surgeons don’t shoot themselves in the chest if they are serious about suicide. The bullet only makes sense if you buy my theory.”

Geopolis: “You’re saying Corrigan shot Donovan and made it look like suicide. Then shot himself. If he had shot himself in the foot, I might accept it. But in the abdomen? Man, that’s a pretty drastic thing to do to produce an alibi.”

Moore: “Not so drastic when you consider the following: he doesn’t eat and has an enema before he shot himself, reducing chance of infection—although he got one anyway. Second, he knows exactly what's in his abdomen and how everything is arranged. He knows because he's a doctor and because he did a study."

"A study?"

"Listen to this. Within a week before the shooting, Corrigan had severe abdominal pain. He insisted on an MRI—a fancy X-ray. You lie on your back and get a picture of your insides, which he then—being on staff—has a long gander at. A day later he reports blood in his stool. Gets a lower GI—barium enema that shows the exact position of his intestinal track lying down. Man ends up knowing more about his insides than bankers know about money."

Geopolis: "But he was shot sitting up. How could he predict how his intestines would be sitting up?"

"Moore: "That's his story, remember. Assume this happened. He shoots his partner, he gets out of the car, lies down, shoots himself, gets back in the car, wipes off the gun, puts the gun in Donovan's hand for prints, calls 911, gets out of the car, lies down again . . ."

Geopolis wasn't impressed. It was too far-fetched. On the other hand, everything about the case was far-fetched. He would have to brief McCabe, and soon.

Before hanging up he said, "You talked to Corrigan's wife after the shooting."

"Yes, the next morning."

"You asked her whether another woman might be involved?"

"Yes. She said no."

"Do me a favor. See her again, soon. Ask about the out-of-town trips. Ask about the Red Lion Inn."

"The Red Lion Inn?"

"The Inn. You might want to show a picture of Corrigan to the desk clerks and bellboys. Ask if they had seen him check in. If so, was he with someone?"

"I'm on my way," Moore said. "There's something else I've been planning to do. There's a guy in town who's known Corrigan since childhood. I'm going to take a long look at Corrigan's past."

"Not too long. Call me the minute you learn anything."

By the time Geopolis would hear from Moore again, TA 131 would be half way across the Atlantic.

Mrs. Corrigan was adamant. Also miffed.

"I told Mr. What's-his-name from the FBI that my husband was faithful. He was faithful. There was no other woman. I would have known."

"What about him being away so much?"

"He had patients, he had meetings. He saw the patients, he went to the meetings. I'm sick of these questions. Can't we talk about something else?"

"The Red Lion. Do you still have the American Express bill?"

"Bob filed it with the other bills. Wherever that is. I'm not going through his things."

Moore got to his feet. Mrs. Corrigan said, "When is Bob coming home?"

"I think the plane arrives around eight. Depending on connections, he should be home by midnight."

Her smile seemed genuine. "I'm so happy," she said.

It was a bellhop at the Red Lion Inn who recognized Corrigan in the snapshot.

"Small fellow?"

"I believe so."

"Had a big hat?"

"I don't know about that," Moore said. "But that's him in the picture?"

"That's him. I saw him check in two or three times. Always at night. I was working nights."

"Was he alone?"

The bellhop laughed. "No sir. He was never alone. He always had a broad with him."

"The same broad?"

"The same broad."

"Can you describe her?"

The bellhop could, and did. He used a lot of adjectives for a bellhop, including gorgeous, fabulous and sexy.

The bellhop could, and did. He used a lot of adjectives for a bellhop, including gorgeous, fabulous and sexy.

9

Three Hours Out

During every oceanic flight, if the weather is smooth, the pilot strolls through the cabin at least once. It's a way to stretch his legs, and is good public relations.

It's particularly good public relations if the captain looked like Donaldson. Grin a mile wide. Teeth from a toothpaste ad. Jimmy Stewart-blue eyes. Crow's feet from squinting into the sun. Swept-back hair with graying temples, 5'10," 180. Fit. A man to trust. A likable man.

Strolling down the aisle, Donaldson chatted with passengers like a good politician, never spending much time with any one passenger, never leaving anyone feeling short-changed. Always someone sitting on the aisle, a pair of baby Johnny Walkers with water back on the fold-down tray—middle-aged, overweight—who might own a hardware store in a small, Midwest town, on vacation with his wife, would say, "Who's minding the store?" And Donaldson would laugh and say, "I thought you were," and the passenger would laugh, and Donaldson would walk on. Some things in life are predictable.

This was different. At one hour out, the plane passed over Stornoway, Scotland. It would be all water until St. Anthony, Newfoundland. This trip through the cabin, Donaldson had no one to chat with except the FBI man and flight attendants. Except, of course, for the passenger in section D.

The man was wearing earphones. His eyes were half-closed and his fingers were tapping in time to the music only he could hear.

He removed his earphones and pushed a button on the Walkman when Donaldson took the seat across the aisle. He looked at Donaldson and waited.

"Mr. Corrigan," Donaldson began, "I've just been talking to our people in New York. They told me some interesting things about you."

Corrigan looked at him.

"For instance, you disappeared from your home in Omaha about five days ago."

No response.

"Your family hasn't heard from you. Guess they're pretty upset. Can you tell me why you did that?"

Corrigan finally spoke. "Is it any of your business?"

"Well, yes," Donaldson said. "I'm responsible for the safety of the plane. There's been a bomb threat. Anything unusual is bound to interest us."

"I didn't make the threat."

"Nobody says you did. But disappearance from home comes in the category of unusual. I would appreciate some explanation."

Corrigan sighed. He picked up his cowboy hat and fiddled with the brim.

"Reason? I told you the reason. I was visiting the wife of Roy Orbison. I'm a fan of her late husband. I wanted to meet her."

Donaldson, incredulous, said, "You mean you left your wife and children and medical practice—without telling anyone—to meet the wife of a country western singer who died years ago?"

"Wasn't that long. And he wasn't country western."

"Had you met her before?"

"No."

"Where does she live?"

"Outside Frankfurt. In Mainz."

"How did you set up the meeting?"

"I read about her in a magazine. I looked up her address in the Mainz phone book. I called her. She agreed to see me. That's all I'm going to say." He started to put back on his earphones when Corrigan reached across the aisle and touched his arm.

"Your family. Why didn't you tell your family?"

"I refuse to say anything more. It really is my business." He put the earphones back in his lap and studied the seat in front of him.

"Okay," Donaldson said. He wondered if he should send the FBI man back to talk with Corrigan.

He went on. "The shooting thing. Tell me about the shooting."

Corrigan looked at Donaldson and smiled.

"Your spies are really on the ball," he said.

"Tell me what happened."

Corrigan said, "You tell me what happened."

Donaldson, fighting back anger, said, "Story is, you had a partner who shot you, then shot himself. The partner died. You got out of the hospital a week ago. That's a pretty Goddamned strange story." Donaldson had let the anger show. "Any reason your partner did this?"

Corrigan shook his head. "No reason. His wife asked a psychiatrist what he thought. He thought my partner had snapped."

On the way to the cockpit, Donaldson took a seat across from the FBI agent/co-pilot. He told him what he had learned from McCabe—the information Geopolis of the FBI had learned by phoning Corrigan's wife. The disguised G-man—his name was Jefferson—knew Geopolis.

"Want me to try?" he asked.

"Won't do any harm," Donaldson said, as he stood and climbed up the stairs to the lounge.

Before going in the cockpit, he took a seat next to his wife, Susan, and told her what happened.

"Should we worry?" Susan asked. Donaldson wasn't sure, but he had the reflexes of an airline pilot.

"Nah. The guy is harmless. Probably a middle-age crisis."

Susan knew pilots, knew the act. "Well, if you're not worried, I'm not. How's Bud?" she asked, referring to the real co-pilot.

"Hasn't said a word since takeoff. The guy hates me. So, let him. Does his job, that's all we ask."

"Well, you can talk to your flight engineer."

"McCoy isn't feeling well. He's not saying anything, but he's gray around the jowls. Going to be a long trip."

"Why don't you stay back here?" Susan asked "We could pet."

"Sounds tempting." Donaldson put his hand on Susan's leg and kissed her on the cheek. He quickly looked around. "Couldn't do that if there were passengers."

Susan put her hand over his. "We could make love and nobody would know."

Donaldson felt stirrings but also embarrassment. "Until Bud or Mac came out to use the john."

He chuckled softly. "The john. Reminds me of a story. Have I told it to you?"

"How would I know unless you tell it?"

"Okay. Back when these lounges were really lounges—before they put in seats—first-class passengers would come up and have a drink before lunch or dinner. Happy hour. Well, on this flight, the hostess says it's time to eat and everybody goes downstairs to their seats except one couple. They ask if they can have another drink before coming down. By letting them, the hostess was breaking a rule, but I guess she was in a good mood because she said okay and went down to start the meal service.

"Half hour later she goes back to the lounge, and guess what? No couple. She was sure they hadn't come back downstairs. Having broken a rule, she felt guilty as well as curious. She goes in the cockpit and tells the captain what happened. 'They have to be somewhere,' she said. He said, 'Is the lav occupied?' She looked at the door and saw the sign was on. She told him it was, in fact, occupied. The captain said, 'Go back down and forget it.'

"Shortly afterward she looked in the cabin and there is the woman, sitting next to her husband. The man was sitting several rows back, alone."

Donaldson paused. "I was the captain," he said.

Susan said, "No, you never told me that story."

The lounge seemed to be getting warmer. They both looked at the lavatory. "Ron," she said. "Please go back to the cockpit. You could be fired for even thinking about what you're thinking."

Nothing was happening in the cockpit. Nothing ever does after reaching cruising altitude until time for descent and landing. Every 40 minutes the co-pilot would call in the plane's position to the nearest ground control. The co-pilot was about to call again. These were the only words the co-pilot had uttered.

For two hours after his second talk with Corrigan, Donaldson sat strapped in the seat, staring at the white sky through his sunglasses. There was only one interruption. Jefferson, the FBI man, had spent some time with Corrigan. He had learned nothing that Donaldson hadn't learned. He said he had instincts about bombers and his instincts told him Corrigan was no bomber.

❦

Donaldson turned around and looked at McCoy. "You okay?"

"I'm fine, Skipper." McCoy didn't look fine. His face glistened with perspiration, although the cockpit was on the cool side. Donaldson decided not to push it. He knew McCoy's history of kidney stones.

He thought of the Fats Waller song, "No one to talk with, nothing to do . . ." Misbehavin' with Susan would be something to do. He resolutely thought of other things.

He thought of bomb threats. Desperate to kill time, he systematically reviewed them in his mind.

The first time a kitchen timer had been used was in a United Airlines DC-4 at Longmont, Colorado in the '50s. A young man had placed the timer in his mother's bag and the dynamite went off about 30 minutes out of Denver. The FBI identified the baggage in which it was placed. They arrested the son within 24 hours. He was convicted and put to death in Colorado.

A more sophisticated timer had been implicated in the PAA 103 crash in Scotland. Probably a cassette radio, PLO suspects.

TWA lost a 707 between Athens and Rome, about 1979, from a bomb planted by terrorists (PLO or PFLP).

Air India lost a 747 off the Irish coast in the mid-'70s. The timer had been defective. Instead of going off in a cargo area on the ground in Japan, it demolished the plane halfway around the world hours later.

Bomb threats have been traced to kids, angry spouses, disgruntled employees, employees of competitors, kooks and extortionists.

TWA had a bomb threat by an extortionist in the mid-70s. He wouldn't identify the flight. He made several phone calls, negotiating for one million down to a hundred thousand in a 12-hour period. TWA refused to concede and the bomb exploded two hours after midnight in the cockpit of a 707 on the ground in Las Vegas. No one was injured.

❦

Then there was D.B. Cooper . . .

Donaldson's ritual for killing time was interrupted by a call from

McCabe. There was a five-way hookup with McCabe in Rockefeller Plaza, dispatch at Kennedy, Interpol in Frankfurt, Donaldson (now three hours outside of Frankfurt) and Geopolis in his FBI office in Washington.

"John." McCabe's voice came over the cockpit speaker. "Steve Geopolis of the FBI has been in touch with a detective named Moore in Omaha. Moore investigated the shooting affair—when allegedly Corrigan's partner shot Corrigan and then killed himself."

"Allegedly?"

"I'll let Steve brief you."

"Captain Donaldson, this is Geopolis of the FBI. A couple of hours ago I talked with Mrs. Corrigan. She told me about her husband's disappearance and the shooting incident. I passed on the information to Mr. McCabe and he called it in to you."

"Right," Donaldson said. "We were about one hour out. John told me what the wife had said."

"Well, now I've talked with an Omaha detective who investigated the case. I'm a little nervous about telling you this, but he has a theory."

Donaldson rested his hands on the useless yoke (the autopilot was doing the flying) and thought, "You're nervous?"

"His theory is that Corrigan killed his partner and then shot himself in the abdomen to escape suspicion."

Donaldson echoed the words back. "In the abdomen? To escape suspicion? The man would have to be crazy."

"Well," Geopolis said, "frankly that's what concerns us. Remember, it's just a theory. But this Omaha detective—Moore, Francis Moore— feels pretty strongly that it's true."

Geopolis then explained why. Partner not suicidal. The miraculous wound. The sluggish slug.

"But mainly hunch," Geopolis said. "Mainly hunch."

There was silence on the five-way hookup. "What happens next?" Donaldson asked.

Moore is talking—right now, I hope—to Corrigan's wife. I think— without much proof—that Corrigan had a girlfriend. Moore also plans to talk to a boyhood friend of Corrigan's someone in Omaha."

McCabe interrupted the Geopolis-Donaldson exchange. "Why the boyhood friend?"

"Moore," Geopolis said, "finds it unbelievable that Corrigan—assuming his theory is correct—would suddenly out of the blue, become a psychopathic killer without something weird in his background."

There didn't seem much else to say.

"Well, keep in touch," Donaldson said, and wondered if they should give more thought to how Corrigan, who might or might not be a psychopath or nut, could have possibly smuggled a bomb on the plane.

10

Corrigan

Jerry Herzog usually took his lunch break at 1 o'clock, but today was Saturday and his boss' lunch break on Saturdays often ran past one. When his boss was away, there was no one but Jerry to wait on customers. He didn't mind. After a long Friday lunch, his boss was usually in a good mood—connected, perhaps, with the gin on his breath—and this pleased Jerry, who liked his boss.

It was 1:35 in Omaha—TA 131 was just south of Iceland—when the phone rang and Jerry answered. The boss was still away.

"Western Auto," he said.

"Mr. Herzog, please."

"Speaking."

"Mr. Herzog, my name is Moore and I'm with the Omaha Police Department. Could I drop by and see you?"

"Good God! What for?"

"Nothing to do with you. I understand you're a friend of Dr. Robert Corrigan. As you may know, Dr. Corrigan has been missing for a few days. We're trying to get some leads."

"Hey, I'm glad to hear that. Not about Bob missing, but . . . you know."

"Nobody has accused you of anything, Mr. Herzog. Just want some background. Understand you've known Dr. Corrigan since you were boys."

"That's right. We grew up together. I still see him from time to time."

"When can we talk?"

"Well, I get off at six. Anytime after that. Evening's free."

"No. It has to be before that. Can I come over now?"

The boss walked in and Jerry said, "Sure, how about McDonald's? I was just leaving for lunch."

"The one on Spruce?"

"That's right. You in uniform?"

"No. How will I recognize you.

"The wheelchair," Jerry said.

❦

McDonald's on Spruce was half a block from Western Auto. Jerry wheeled himself down the street and up the ramp for the disabled. His wheelchair was pulled up at a red plastic-topped table when Moore walked in the door. There were no other wheelchairs. Moore pulled up a chair.

"Looks good," he said.

"Quarter-pounder, fries, Diet Coke. I usually don't get fries. You're Mr. Moore?"

"Francis Moore," Moore said and held out a hand to be shaken. Herzog had a muscular forearm and a strong grip. He had a flat belly, white shirt and tie. He had a round, pleasant face. His legs were lifeless and too thin for his body.

There was no time for pleasantries. "Tell me about Corrigan," Moore said.

"Tell you what?"

"What kind of kid was he?"

"Like any kid. Maybe a little quieter . . . a little more shy. But he could be tough in a fight. Where we grew up you had to be tough."

"Where was that?"

"Olpe, Kansas. Little farm town near Emporia. Mostly Germans. Bob was raised by his German grandmother. His folks were dead. Car accident, I think."

Moore was familiar with the details of the bomb threat. "Does that mean he spoke German?"

"He spoke German before he spoke English. His grandmother hardly knew any English."

"How was he in school?"

"Smartest in the class. 'Course it was a small class. But he was smart in college. Still smart—smartest doc in Omaha."

Herzog poured ketchup on his fries. "Always wondered why we got along. He was smart, I was dumb. He became a surgeon, I clerk at Western Auto. But every few weeks he comes in the store, often around lunchtime. We've shared many a chocolate shake."

"What do you talk about?"

"The weather. Hell, I don't know. Bob was never a talker. Me neither. Maybe that's why we got along."

"Did he ever get in trouble? As a kid?"

"Too smart to get in trouble. There wasn't anybody in Olpe better behaved. Small town, of course."

"But no sissy?"

"No. If he'd been a sissy, I might not be in a wheelchair."

For all his hurry, Moore had to swallow a couple of times before he could talk.

"You'll have to explain," he finally said.

Herzog pushed himself back from the table and wiped his mouth with a paper napkin.

"Ever play chicken when you were a kid?"

Moore shook his head, not knowing for certain what the truthful answer was.

"We did, Bob and me. Bob loved to play chicken with trains."

"Trains?"

"You know, hop a train, cross the platform, and hop off the other side. Or ride it a few hundred yards and bail out before it gets moving too fast."

"Good way to get a little bit hurt."

"Great thing about playing chicken with trains. Either you make it or you don't. You don't get a little bit hurt."

Herzog grinned and rolled his eyes. "Of course, I had to be the exception."

Moore understood. "That's why you're in a wheelchair."

"It was summer in Olpe. Bob and I were eleven. We loved trains. Used to hang around the train yard, watch the older kids trying to hop freights as a game. Bob said, 'Let's try it.' We tried it. Bob hopped off. I fell off. Just my luck, to be the exception. Just got a little bit hurt."

He seemed to enjoy telling the story.

"Looks like you were quite a bit hurt."

"Spinal injury. Could have been worse."

Herzog stared out the window at the McDonald's playground. "You know, for days afterwards I thought I had been pushed. But Bob would never do that."

Moore couldn't believe his ears. When he finally spoke, it came out raspy.

"Why do you think you were pushed."

"No reason, really. In the hospital I was feeling sorry for myself. I had to blame somebody. I imagined things. I imagined standing on the platform, waiting to hop off, and something, a gust of air, maybe, threw me off-balance."

"Possibly a hand?"

"Maybe."

"And Bob was the only one around?"

"He may have hopped off first. I don't remember."

"But you suspected Bob of pushing you?"

"Maybe. For a time."

"Not now?"

"I told you. It was my imagination. Bob was my closest friend. His grandmother paid my hospital bills. My family was poor as dirt. We exchange Christmas cards. We eat in here and who usually pays? Bob."

Moore didn't know what to say, so he said, "Well, I'm sure you're right. Bob doesn't seem like that kind of person."

Herzog had to return to work and Moore had to make a call. He had time for one question.

"You said Bob liked to play chicken. Ever know him to play chicken in other ways?"

Herzog was turning his wheelchair around to leave. He stopped and seemed to focus on the condiment stand.

"I heard a story I don't know is true. Bob was out west somewhere during a college break. There was a party, a lot of beer drinking. Apparently, Bob had gotten a hold of some sticks of dynamite. While his friends were partying indoors he was outdoors arranging the sticks in a circle. Then he yelled for his friends to come out and see what he was doing.”

Moore knew how the story would end. It was the oldest of macho stunts.

“Bob stood in the middle of the circle. He lit a long fuse connected to a stick of dynamite. I’m not sure how it all works, but if all the sticks explode at the same time, the person in the middle isn’t hurt. If some go off before others, the person is blown to smithereens. Something to do with physics. It’s one hell of a gamble.”

“Believe the story?”

Herzog thought it over and said, “Yes, I believe I do.”

Corrigan’s secretary was a brunette with tinted glasses. Moore introduced himself. She didn’t seem surprised. Probably some other policemen had questioned her about the two partners—one dead, one missing—whom she had worked for.

“I really have only one question,” Moore said. “It’s about women. I assume Dr. Corrigan knows many women.”

“I would say so.”

“Patients in and out?”

“Yes.”

“And, here, at a teaching hospital, students, residents? Other faculty? Other secretaries besides yourself?”

“Yes, of course, what are you trying to say?”

“Please, think, Ms. . . .”

“Higgins,” she said.

“Did Corrigan—does Corrigan—know any women of outstanding beauty, a real . . .” He searched for the right word and couldn’t find it. “. . . bimbo?”

Silence. Moore searched for other words. Ms. Higgins clearly hadn’t liked bimbo.

“Many women are attractive, Ms. Higgins. I’m thinking of a woman who is very attractive. Super attractive. . .”

She waited.

“Someone you might describe as gorgeous . . . fabulous . . . sexy?”

She suddenly smiled. “Gorgeous? Fabulous? Sexy? You must be thinking of Julia Guedet.”

Moore was euphoric. "Who is Julia Guedet?"

"A young German woman. She was a radiology resident until about six months ago. I think she went back to Germany . . ."

"How did Dr. Corrigan know her?"

"Well, because she came in the office so often. For a while, every day."

"To look at X-rays?"

"Yes, I suppose so."

"Any other reason?"

She hesitated. "Well, who can say? Maybe they did more than look at X-rays."

"She and Dr. Corrigan?"

"No. She and Dr. Donovan."

Yes, the Department of Radiology had the address of Dr. Julia Guedet. She had finished her residency on Jan. 1. She lived at 31 Willemstrasse, Frankfurt.

11

Four Hours Out

For a jetliner crossing the Atlantic at 35,000 feet in the daytime, the sun remains motionless throughout the flight: a bright glob suspended at a fixed angle in the overhead sky. Flying westward was a race with the sun. At 600 miles per hour, the plane would lose the race, but it would be close. When they left Frankfurt, it was late afternoon; it would be dusk when they landed at Dulles. At 35,000 feet they could see the earth's curvature. When they descended the earth became flat again and the sun would sink in the west.

The flight had been smooth: an occasional light chop. The jetstreams eased off over water. There would be more chops, harder chops, when they approached Canada where the jetstreams were stronger. They often felt the chops before they saw land.

TA 131 had just passed the southern tip of Greenland. The bright tundra was plainly visible off the right wing tip. Icebergs shown brilliantly on the surface of the becalmed water. Ninety percent of the icebergs below the surface turn from turquoise to royal blue at greater depths. A colorful, serene sight from 35,000 feet.

Donaldson had studied the spectacle many times but he had never lost his appreciation for it. The aesthetics did not blind him to the impersonal cruelty of icebergs. The Titanic had been a victim of one and had sunk just a few miles south of their flight path.

Donaldson heard the co-pilot call in their position report to Gander Oceanic control. As the plane banked, not too gently, setting course for Stephenville, Newfoundland, Donaldson felt a moment of irritation. Autopilots usually do a smoother job. Donaldson liked the course changes that were less detectable to passengers. He took pride in his reputation as a "smooth pilot." A rough autopilot maneuver was a personal affront. This was the fourth position report to Oceanic control since starting across the Atlantic. It had been four hours since takeoff and the only words Donaldson had heard from Fowler were the position reports. He looked off to his right at the Davis Strait and wondered whether he should comment on Fowler's silence. He decided against it. If the man hated him, he hated him.

❧

The interphone rang. It was Susan calling from the upper lounge.

"Ron, you'd better come back." He winced. She knew he didn't like to be called Ron with others listening; it must be serious or she would have remembered.

Susan was sitting next to a good-looking attendant whose name Donaldson had forgotten or never known. Susan looked grim. The attendant looked frantic. What now?

"She says she knows where the bomb is," Susan said softly.

Donaldson's heart skipped a beat while she struggled to appear calm. "Is she sure? How does she know?"

"She says it's behind a panel downstairs."

"How does she know?"

"Someone told her."

"Someone?"

"A voice."

Donaldson felt the tension slip away. He looked at the attendant sympathetically. "What's your name?"

"Lois Lister. I'm from Buffalo."

"A voice told you there was a bomb?"

She nodded, her mascara-fringed eyes wide and frightened-looking.

"When did it tell you?"

"Just before I came on the plane. It told me exactly where the bomb was."

"And where was that?"

"Behind the panel under the phone. The phone by the door where you come in. The L-1 door."

"Have you told anyone besides Susan?"

"I told Susan because I know she's your wife. You must warn the crew

77

about the bomb. The crew should know."

"Did the voice tell you when the bomb would go off?"

"Yes. Somewhere over Greenland. Where no one could survive a crash." She seemed less frantic and more matter-of-fact, but Donaldson still felt wary. Susan was goggle-eyed.

Then," Donaldson said, "we should do something right away. Let's go down. Lois, you can show us the panel."

Donaldson got a screwdriver from the cockpit and they walked down the spiral staircase.

"Here," Lois said. She pointed under the phone lodged in the stub bulkhead, just feet from the lounge staircase, at the L-1 door.

Donaldson leaned over and then got to his knees. The outline of the inspection panel was barely visible. He began unscrewing screws.

The panel fell free of its casing. Inside there was a tangle of multi-colored wires, related to the public address system, inside a shallow space. There was nothing resembling a bomb.

He motioned to Lois to look into the space. "Do you see anything, Lois? Do you see a bomb?"

Lois looked puzzled. She didn't seem relieved. She seemed . . . disappointed.

"Perhaps," Donaldson said, we should go back upstairs."

Susan and Lois sat in two seats and Donaldson sat across the aisle.

"Lois, please understand that I'm the captain of the plane and I need your help. How long have you been hearing voices?"

Lois looked drained. Her beautiful face was pale and drawn. She seemed to lack the energy to respond.

"Since I stopped sleeping," she finally said.

"And when was that? When did you stop sleeping?"

"I can't remember. It's been days and days. I haven't slept for days."

"Did you sleep last night?"

"I couldn't. I couldn't read or watch television. I spent the whole night walking in the park."

"All night? Weren't you afraid?"

"No. I didn't care. I thought, let him kill me. I didn't care."

"How long has this not caring gone on?"

Lois, without warning, burst into tears.

"Since they told me," she said. "Since they told me they would have to . . . remove my breast. That I had cancer."

The crying got worse and Susan put her arm around Lois' shoulder. Donaldson went to the lavatory and brought back some tissues.

"You've been pretty depressed," he said.

She blew her nose on the tissue and nodded.

"Well, we'll look after you. Susan, do we have any Valium in the medical kit?"

Susan went to the front of the lounge and rummaged through a drawer.

"There's a stethoscope and some nitroglycerin tablets. No Valium."

"Just take it easy," Lois," Donaldson said. "We'll be in Washington in a few hours. A doctor will be waiting at the airport."

"Why wasn't there a bomb?" Lois moaned. "I was so hoping for a bomb."

"Susan will stay up here with you," Donaldson said.

Finally, Susan would have something to do on this one-passenger flight.

❧

Donaldson had just walked in the cockpit door when he heard McCabe's voice on the speaker.

"One thirty one? McCabe here. Plus Kennedy. Plus Frankfurt. Plus Mr. Geopolis of the FBI. Plus—I think, wait a minute—I believe a patch-in from Omaha. Detective Francis Moore in Omaha? Are you there? Lieutenant Moore?"

"I'm here." Moore's voice was as clear as McCabe's. McCabe explained, "Mr. Geopolis thought that since Lieutenant Moore got the story he should tell it. What did you learn, Lieutenant?"

"I talked to a man named Jerry Herzog who had known Corrigan when they were kids. He described Corrigan as normal in every way except he liked to play chicken."

"Play chicken?" somebody said.

"Play chicken with trains. Hop on a moving freight. Hop off. See who can stay on the track the longest before the train gets there. That sort of thing."

There was silence on the six-way hookup.

"One day Corrigan and his friend Herzog were playing chicken on a moving freight train. Corrigan hopped off safely. Herzog fell off. He survived but was crippled. Stuck in a wheelchair ever since . . .

"Nice guy," he added. "Doesn't believe Corrigan pushed him off the train. Believed it once, but now believes he was wrong. Corrigan's a nice guy too. Too nice to be pushing friends off trains."

"Wow!" someone said.

"Something else," Moore said. "Story going around that Corrigan once pulled the old dynamite trick. You know, stand in the middle of a circle of dynamite sticks? If they all go off together, you live. If they go off singly, you die. The ultimate in chicken."

Silence on the six-way hookup. McCabe: "Anything else?"

Moore: "The bellhop at the Red Lion Inn, here in Omaha, saw Corrigan check in several evenings with what the bellhop called a gorgeous babe. She is also fabulous—big word for a bellhop—and sexy."

"Aha!" someone said.

"Corrigan's secretary thinks she knows who the bellhop was talking about. Someone named Julia Guedet. G-U-E-D-E-T. She was a resident in radiology at the medical center where Corrigan—and his late partner, Donovan—worked. Came to the office often. Very cozy with one of them. Guess which one?"

Nobody tried.

"Donovan, the partner who shot Corrigan in the tummy and then himself in the heart. Except I don't believe it."

McCabe: "We understood you didn't believe it. What do you think now?"

"I think we should get hold of Julia Guedet, pronto. She lives in Frankfurt. I have the address."

Interpol cut in. "Let me have it," said the well-bred English voice. "We'll send somebody right out."

"Better hurry," Moore said. "Believe me, this guy looks very suspicious. You'd better be thinking how he might have gotten a bomb on board."

Donaldson filled in the FBI agent dressed as a co-pilot. "Think he got through security with something?" he asked.

"Plastic, perhaps. Metal, no. Let me suggest something. Ask Interpol to check out the guard who interrogated Donaldson. He's got a carryon bag with him. I'll go through it—really go through it. What about a body search?"

Donaldson considered the idea and discarded it.
"Let's wait to hear what Julia says. Too bad we can't get in the cargo hold. That may be the bag we should be checking."

The security guard who had checked Corrigan was still on duty. He remembered Corrigan, his cowboy hat and the puzzling story about a girlfriend who was a doctor but worked at the Air Force base.

He repeated the story to Interpol. Interpol repeated it to Donaldson. Donaldson swore. "That son of a bitch," he said. "He told me he was visiting Roy Orbison's wife. Which story is true?"

He thought it over. "Going on what Moore tells us, I guess the Julia story makes more sense. But why would the bastard lie to me?"

Moore was back on the cabin speaker, the six-way conference call arranged again by the Kennedy dispatcher.

"Forgot one thing. May be important."

"Let's hear it," McCabe said.

"Our friend Corrigan speaks German. Raised by a German grandmother. Speaks perfect German."

"Interesting," someone said.

"Particularly," McCabe said, "since the bomb caller spoke perfect German."

It was a flight for medical emergencies, if you consider Lois Lister's psychotic depression medical.

Now it was McCoy. He was bent almost double over his desktop facing the instrument panel.

And then, seeing Donaldson, he did something typical of McCoy. He told a joke. "Know why the FAA fired a 70-year-old hostess? Found structural damage?"

Donaldson didn't laugh. At the moment, nothing would have made him laugh. For the first time, he had begun to believe that there really was a bomb on board and that the little man in section D had brought it.

81

A loud noise, a hole in the fuselage, a plane spinning out of control. He considered descending to a lower altitude, perhaps 10,000 feet; the cabin wouldn't be pressurized and a bomb would cause less damage. But at that altitude he wouldn't have enough fuel to make it to Dulles. He thought of Susan and his children, his good life. For a split second he felt fear. But it passed as he contemplated what to do with McCoy.

"Dammit, McCoy, you've been passing stones for years. Why the hell does the AME let you fly?"

Mac groaned. "He's an old buddy. We got a conspiracy going. I won't tell on him, he won't tell on me." He groaned again. Donaldson wondered what goods McCoy had on the medical examiner. He would never find out.

Unless McCoy recovered quickly, Donaldson faced losing one-third of his crew. Another third—Bud, the co-pilot—was so pissed off, Donaldson wasn't sure he could count on him either.

Donaldson went looking for medicine kits. There were supposed to be three of them. There were three all right. One contained two syringes, a vial of epinephrine and some cotton balls. Another contained an instruction book for dealing with in-flight medical emergencies. Donaldson already knew what the third contained—a stethoscope and nitroglycerin tablets.

Incredibly there was no morphine, no Demerol, no Percodan. Nothing to relieve the agony of a sharp-edged stone passing through a tube the size of a soda straw.

"I have some aspirin," the male purser said. "Would that help?" Donaldson gazed at the purser. The purser had accompanied him on the search. A purser, he recalled, had given AIDS to half of San Francisco. The whole city? Just the gay part? Or were the two the same? Donaldson hated all pursers at the moment.

He proceeded to lecture the only purser available.

"Did you know there are 3,000 in-flight medical emergencies annually? Did you know that medical care of passengers who become ill during flights has been a concern since the early days of commercial aviation? Do you know . . ." He paused for breath . . . "that in 1986 the FAA instituted new regulations requiring certain medical supplies aboard all U.S. aircraft capable of carrying 30 or more passengers?"

The purser didn't flinch. He counterattacked. "If you know those things," he said tartly, "you know that neither morphine nor any other powerful analgesic was included in what the FAA called the new enhanced medical kit. The drugs would have a survival life of one half hour—no lock has been designed that would protect them."

The purser wasn't finished. "You must also know that 450 million fly annually in the U.S. alone. A medical kit is needed once in every 1,900 flights, or one use for every 150,000 air travelers. It's not surprising that oversights occur."

"Oversights!" Donaldson was turning purple. "Up front the chances of a single instrument being defective may be one in a trillion, but we check every instrument every time we fly. You—the purser— should check the medicine kits." He stopped short of asking the purser's name. Maybe it wasn't the purser's job to check medicine kits.

The purser had the last word. "I agree about the inadequacy of medicine kits in most aircraft. What concerns me more than missing items is the inferior quality of items in the enhanced medical kit—possibly the result of an uninformed zeal for economy by the air carrier. Consider that stethoscope upstairs in the lounge. How useful would it be if we had a flight that was normally full? Let me tell you."

Donaldson felt his anger subside. The purser had at least given medicine kits some thought.

"It's hard to imagine a more crowded, noisy examining room than an aircraft cabin. The ambient noise levels on board a commercial aircraft generally are low frequency (less than 4,000 Hz, range upward of 65 dB, and may approach 90 dB during climb). At these levels, no stethoscope is sensitive enough to pick up arterial sounds, although it adequately transmits extraneous cabin and engine noise."

The purser looked around the cabin. "Today's flight," he said., "may be an exception. Maybe you could hear something through a stethoscope."

❧

Donaldson had to restrain himself from breaking into a run to escape the pedantic purser. Back in the cockpit, he said, "Mac, apparently there's nothing on board that will help your pain. Are you going to make it?"

McCoy was still bent over his desktop, but he seemed to be breathing easier.

"Don't worry about me, Skipper. I'll be 100 percent when you need me." Donaldson patted him on the shoulder and sat down in the left-hand seat. He glanced over at Bud in the right-hand seat. The co-pilot still was not talking. Then Donaldson smelled something that surprised him. He could have sworn it was garlic.

Garlic was a standing joke in cockpits. Donaldson remembered numerous times, when flying out of Madrid, he had smelled the garlic of Tosca's. His usual line was, "Next time take me with you."

But you always smelled the garlic early in the flight. After a mercifully short time it would dissipate. They had been served lunch in the cockpit, but airplane lunches never contain garlic for obvious reasons.

This was garlic. Donaldson was sure. Who had been eating garlic? He looked at the co-pilot and a horrible thought crossed his mind.

12

Julia

Frankfurt
11:26 p.m. Friday

Interpol's report on Julia Guedet (relayed to Interpol headquarters by a woman operative from a car phone outside Julia's apartment):

Julia Guedet is your typical Rhinemaiden—athletic, strong, clean, healthy. She is a very liberated young woman. She has a casual, liberal view of sex as something that is done to relieve tension. You do it as you wish. It doesn't need to involve a commitment of any type.

Julia went to Omaha because the family has relatives there and she felt this would be a way to travel and improve her English. She applied to the University of Nebraska Medical School and received a residency appointment in the Department of Radiology. She met both Donovan and Corrigan and was attracted to them. Both were good looking in their own way and she had a little hospital fling with both of them. Donovan was just a little off-the-cuff business in the linen closet one night. She pretended to like Donovan more than Corrigan—to throw people off—but she slept more with Corrigan. Apparently it meant a lot more to Corrigan than it did to Julia. He's very jealous of Donovan without cause, it seems, except for the linen closet.

Julia's chairman has connection with the SAC base in Omaha and through him she did some moonlighting at the SAC hospital. It's her connection with SAC that led to her job with the Air Force base next to the Frankfurt airport. Her job consists of working on new ways of detecting plastic materials used for bombs.

85

On a personal level, she and Corrigan had a much bigger affair than she had with Donovan, but it isn't what she would call a real affair. They went to a hotel several times. Probably two dozen times they actually went to bed together. She does not put much emphasis on the affair. It was just a sexual exercise as far as she was concerned.

She goes back to Germany. She's working in Germany and she hears through friends in Omaha about the assault-suicide of Corrigan and Donovan. This upsets her very much because as far as she was concerned, Donovan was very easy-going, not the type to do this sort of thing. Corrigan she is not too sure about. She doesn't understand how he might have engineered this, but she feels very uneasy about the shooting and feels that she might have had something to do with it.

Six weeks later, Corrigan shows up on her doorstep. This is *very* upsetting. She realizes by now she is dealing with a man who is maybe not a true psychopath, but is certainly not dealing with a full deck. But he's here, they do a little sightseeing, they sleep together, they eat at a couple of nice restaurants. Then he tells her he wants to leave his wife and children and marry her.

Of course, she has no intention of doing anything like this. She doesn't love him, there was never any question of loving him, but she is afraid to be too abrupt with him for fear that she might trigger something in him. She tries to let him down gently. She tells him she is very fond of him, but that she could not live with his leaving his wife, whom she feels he really is fond of, and his children, whom she knows he is very fond of. She tells him she cannot be the instigator of breaking up his home. She says she cannot live in the United States, must live in Germany, doesn't think he really wants to live in Germany. She says she thinks before they go any further this is a good time to break it off.

They hadn't seen each other now for months because she had finished her residency the first of January, so she said I really think we ought to cut it off now and remain friends. She told him he would always hold a very special place in her heart, but she really didn't want to marry him. "I cannot marry you if it is going to tear up your family. I just can't do this."

Corrigan seems not too pleased with this, but seems to accept it and agrees that maybe he was being a little rash to come running over here. Several things have happened recently that have upset him and maybe this is why he did it.

And so they proceed to have one last day. They do a little more sightseeing and have a nice dinner and then he says he would like to see where she worked before going back, so they arrange for the next day, their last day, to take him out to see her lab. In the meantime, Corrigan's attitude is pleasant, cheerful, a little subdued. She's congratulating herself on his not having gotten angry or morose or out of hand in any way. He seemed to be taking it well, but she says to herself that she will be very, very happy when he takes off and goes back home. She really *feels* like she is sitting on a powder keg dealing with this man.

Anyway, they go out to the base and with her clearance she gets him in and of course he not only is a cardiovascular surgeon but he has always been interested in things scientific and understands very well, unlike some medical doctors, research and the jargon, so they spend an enjoyable morning touring the labs and she shows him what they are working on and he shows a lot of interest, asks a lot of question and she shows him at one point the different types of plastics that they are using. There is one special plastic which is very, very potent, has a lot of explosive power in a very small volume, and this is the one they are being particularly cautious about because they are trying to find some way they can detect it.

Anyway, everything is all very pleasant and then he asks her if he can use the phone. He says he needs to call the airport and confirm his reservation. She says sure. She takes him into her office where the plastic was kept. Where they had been earlier and had seen the plastic. She looks up the number for him at the airport and leaves him there. She says as long as he was going to be on the phone, she would do a quick errand down the hall. So she leaves him alone in the lab with the telephone.

When she comes back, they go out and have a lovely dinner and bittersweet sexual encounter. The next morning she wakes up and knows he is leaving and has mixed feelings—doesn't want to check

and make sure he's leaving but does want to. She knows what time his
plane is leaving, so she goes out to the airport and she stands out of
the way where she can see the entrance and she watches and she waits
and she sees him come in and she sees him go over to the international desk and from there down to the international sterile area and then
she goes up to the observation deck. The plane is several hours late
taking off but she still waits. In her own mind she is very uneasy and
feels she cannot leave the airport until the airplane has left the ground
and this man is safely out of her life.

Interpol at Frankfurt asked the female operative: "Corrigan was alone
with the explosive?"

"Yes."

"While he was calling the airport?"

"Yes."

"Was any of the explosive missing?"

"Silence from the car phone. "I don't know. I didn't ask."

"You'd better check."

"She's in her apartment. I'll check right now."

"By the way, would you describe this woman as beautiful?"

The operative—an Englishwoman and suspected lesbian—hesitated a
moment. "Men might find her so," she said.

Second report to Interpol:

I went back to the apartment and said to Julia, "You mentioned
that you showed him some explosives. And he was alone with it?"
She says, "Ach mein Gott, yes. When he made the phone call. I think
we'd better check and see if there's any missing."

So we get in my car and go speeding across Frankfurt and out to
the lab and she says it will take a few minutes to check the various
supplies. She comes back from the office and her face is ashen and
she is kind of trembling and she says, "My God, there are two ounces
of XC6/32 missing." I say, "Is that important? Is that very potent?"
She says, "Well, it could blow a pretty good sized hole in the side of a
747. It's less than two ounces. You could hide it anywhere."

I ask, "Anything else missing?" She says, "The 1812 Overture." I thought maybe she had cracked under the strain. "What do you mean the 1812 Overture?" She said, "It's a cassette tape of the 1812 Overture and when you get to the part at the end where the cannons go off, that was the detonator for the plastic . . ."

89

13

Six Hours Out

From the Greenland tundra to Cape Cod is 1,580 nautical miles and three hours of flying time in a 747 at 35,000 feet. In his 29 years of flying, Donaldson had never gone through a three-hour period more—in the airman's language of understatement—challenging.

First was the near air collision. It followed a personal collision between Donaldson and the co-pilot. A short digression on the INS is needed for background.

INS is short for Intertial Navigation System. It's the same system that managed flight to the moon and back. With the INS, accuracy of aircraft position is instantly determined—within tenths of nautical miles and tenths of a minute—in resolving the age-old problems of time and distance in navigation. With three INS units a triple redundancy system exists when even a failure of one unit is a rarity.

The beauty of the INS lies in it being totally self-contained. Ground equipment is not required. It cannot be sabotaged.

Each INS is aligned to a plane's first position on the ground before takeoff. Computers then account for any changes of position due to movement in direction or distance. Constant readouts tell crews not only where they are but how fast they got there and how long it will take them to get where they want to go.

There is still room for human error. Positions must be programmed into the computer along the route. A mistake can cause the plane to fly off course or head for the wrong destination. This is what happened to Korean Airlines 007 and the disastrous mistake of the Russians in shooting it down.

Autopilots receive input from the INS, then steer the plane with the crew acting as little more than observers. Their task is simply to program the three computers with latitude and longitude numbers along their intended course.

Four and a half hours out of Frankfurt—more than half way home—Donaldson had a rare moment of something resembling relaxation. Steady on course, approaching land fall, all systems go: maybe his concerns had been unwarranted. McCoy was no longer grating his teeth; the co-pilot's garlic breath was worrisome but his stony silence a blessing. Donaldson decided to revisit the cabin. "Keep an eye on things," he told Mac. He had as little desire to speak to the co-pilot as the co-pilot had to speak to him. Tightening his tie, donning his jacket from the coat rack in the bunk area, Donaldson straightened his hat in the mirror on the cockpit bulkhead door and left.

The sole occupant in the upper lounge was Jefferson, the FBI agent posing as a deadheading three-striper co-pilot. Donaldson wondered why he had moved there. He also wondered where Susan and the hallucinating attendant had gone.

"If you're bored," he told the FBI man, "take my seat. Maybe the co-pilot will need some help."

"Thanks. I've got a private license. If it hadn't been for law school and the bureau, I might have had your job."

"Be my guest. Mac will explain things to you. I'll be back shortly."

Donaldson descended the spiral stairs to the main cabin deck to look for Susan. He found her sitting across the aisle from Lois Lister in coach. Lois was stretched out under a blanket along a row of seats with her eyes closed. This was the advantage of coach: you could put down the arm rests and snooze for the whole trip if there weren't too many passengers. Today there weren't too many.

Donaldson smiled reassuringly at Susan and walked on back through the cabin.

E cabin in a 747 is the farthest aft of five cabins. The tail experiences the greatest oscillation in choppy air. Because of its distance from the wing center of gravity, it's like the end of a rope in a crack-the-whip game.

The plane lurched side to side in a fish-tail fashion. Passengers might have attributed this to turbulence, but Donaldson knew better. There was some disturbance in the flight control system—perhaps the autopilot had been disconnected. If so, why?

He cut short his chatter with the attendants. Walking quickly, he started the long trek to the A cabin. Going up the spiral stairs, he had to hold onto the railing.

Jefferson, the FBI agent, was still in the lounge. In the cockpit, Donaldson saw the co-pilot leaning over the INS units and fumbling with the autopilot controls on the glare shield.

"What goes?"

"Got a little rough, so I'm correcting back on manual control. Autopilot's a little jerky on this bird."

"Are we off-course?"

"Okay, Captain, blame me. I bumped the controls and knocked the autopilot off. When I reconnected it, I didn't put it back on INS mode. My fault. You're entirely right to blame me, Captain."

Donaldson flipped his hat on the bunk and mounted his seat. He still had his jacket on, something unusual when he flew.

It called for fast action. Canadian Airways was not forgiving of excursion off-course. Before long, they would send out RCAF interceptions. This would not only excite the passengers (correction: passenger) but probably make the news.

Gander traffic control acknowledged TA 131 on radar and accepted Donaldson's explanation without comment. There would be a report. Donaldson dreaded the debriefing at Dulles.

Donaldson noticed something. The garlic smell was gone. Now there was another smell. A small familiar smell. Leaning over to greet a passenger drinking his second vodka martini, Donaldson had smelled the smell hundreds of times.

Bud had been drinking. He was sure of it. Anger was followed by disgust, then apprehension. Bud had bumped into the controls. What else would he bump into?

Donaldson felt an urgent need to get Fowler out of the cockpit. He would have liked to manage it gracefully, but wasn't sure how.

Donaldson turned to McCoy and said, "Mac, you're looking worse than ever. Why don't you go back to the lounge and stretch out between two seats? Just until you feel a little better." He winked at McCoy and nodded toward the cockpit door. Without saying anything, McCoy left the seat and went into the lounge, closing the door behind him.

Donaldson looked at Bud hunched forward in his seat. "How much have you had?" he asked. Fowler looked straight ahead, his face a mask. "Had what, Captain?"

"You know what. I can smell it on your breath."

"Bullshit, Captain."

"That's why you bumped the controls. What am I going to do with you?"

Fowler turned his head and looked at Donaldson. His face was slightly flushed, but his eyes were clear. He grinned mischievously.

"That's your problem, Captain. I haven't had a drink in 16 months."

Donaldson almost exploded with anger. "Maybe sixteen months until today. Why did you choose today?"

"Choose what, Captain?"

"To drink, you bastard."

"Screw you, Captain." He looked at Donaldson and added, "You screwed my father, you screwed me. When will you give up, Captain?"

"Bud, you can't drink and fly."

"Prove I've been drinking. Do you have a breathalyzer?"

At first Donaldson only had Fowler's breath to go on. Anyone could bump a control. But now Fowler sounded drunk. If he kept drinking, he would become a belligerent drunk. This could be a bigger problem for the safety of the plane than a bomb that wasn't there.

"Okay, Bud. Take it easy. You're right. I can't prove anything. But I have my nose. You've got a helluva problem, fella."

"Bullshit," Bud repeated.

"Now your problem is my problem." He wondered if Fowler had any little bottles in his pockets. There were no bulges that he could see. He wondered if he should frisk him. He decided not to. You could hide the little bottles anywhere.

Donaldson picked up the interphone and asked for Susan. He told her to come to the cockpit. "Get another attendant to sit with Lois."

When she cracked the door and looked in, Donaldson said, "Bud's been drinking. He denies it, but I'm sure of it."

"Jesus," she said.

"You have a new assignment. You're to sit in the lounge with Bud. I'm not letting him stay in the cockpit."

Susan stared at Bud, whose chin had sunk to his chest. "Bud, is it true?"

Bud didn't answer. Donaldson said, "Bud, go back to the lounge with Susan. Susan, order up some coffee. Never take your eyes off of him. It's possible he hasn't had much to drink. It's possible that I'll need him later."

"Ron," she said. "This is terrible."

"I know," he said. "Ask them to bring me some coffee too."

Donaldson seethed. A sick flight engineer, a soused co-pilot. What else could go wrong. Oh yes, a bomb could explode at any minute.

Donaldson heard McCoy come back in the cockpit and settle into his flight engineer seat. McCoy must know what was going on. Neither said a word.

Time now for the INS. How far was the plane off track? Donaldson started doing computations. The plane was badly off track. There was no time for a smooth correction. The plane needed to be turned to the left and it wouldn't be smooth.

Donaldson banked the craft sharply while scanning his left turn for traffic. Over the North Atlantic, one doesn't expect much traffic. This was not a trip for the expected, however. He caught a glimpse of flashing metal. What started as a not-too-gentle maneuver became an aerobatic gyration when he forcibly overcontrolled the autopilot into a dive. A shiny 767 disappeared overhead.

If there had been time, Donaldson would have worried about whether his 65-foot vertical fin would clear the path of the 767, which had taken no evasive action. There hadn't been time. The two planes glided past each other with perhaps 100 feet to spare.

"Missed him," Mac blurted, holding onto his desktop to keep from being pitched to the cockpit ceiling from the sudden dive. Already ashen white, Mac groaned as a hot knife-like pain shot through his groin. He apologized for the groan. "Sorry, Skipper, but your outside loop must have knocked a gem loose in my plumbing. Hurts like hell."

A delayed reaction was setting in and Donaldson couldn't think of anything to say. The interphone rang and Susan asked, "For God's sake, what's going on?"

"Near miss," Donaldson managed to say.

"How near?"

"Near enough to flutter your eyebrows. How's our co-pilot?"

"The same. We both managed to stay in our seats."

"Call the purser, will you?" Donaldson said. "See if everybody downstairs is okay."

The phone rang a minute later and Susan said, "Not a scratch, not a bruise. But try not to do something like that again, okay?"

"I promise," Donaldson said.

The passenger was singing alone with his Walkman. Freda VanValkenburg, sitting beside him, heard "dum dum dum dum-bedoo-wah." Her curiosity got the best of her. She tapped him on the shoulder.

He took off his earphones and peered around the seat. "Hello," he said.

"Hi there," she said. "Is that Bruce Springsteen?"

"No, Roy Orbison. 'Only the Lonely.' But you're close. Springsteen and Roy were friends and sometimes wrote the same kind of songs. Roy's songs were darker. He always wrote about some kind of loss that seemed, well, unbearable."

"I like Roy Orbison," Freda said.

"You do?" The passenger smiled happily. "Why don't you sit across the aisle so we can talk? I don't meet many Orbison fans."

She sat across the aisle. "I'm not sure fan is the word," she said. "I like Tom Petty better. I like Merle Haggard."

"Both are tremendous," the passenger said. "My name's Bob Corrigan. What's yours?"

Freda told him and said, "I particularly like 'In Dreams.'"

"It's an extraordinary song," Corrigan agreed. "It's five or six melodies tied together. It breaks all the rules of pop music. Any other favorites?"

Freda thought about it. "I've got Orbison's album . . . I forget the name. I like 'Coming Home.'"

"The Class of '55. Johnny Cash and Jerry Lee Lewis were having a reunion with Roy. Orbison is great in 'Coming Home.' The song has a spiritual quality. Reminds us that everyone dies."

Freda really hadn't listened to the words, but liked the tune.

"A lonely man in black singing about lost loves and midnight fears."

"Did you make that up?" Freda asked.

"I'm quoting from 'Rolling Stone.' 'The pure, aching melancholy, the burst of passion that was invariably called 'operatic' . . . night after night, he'd take the stage, stand dead still in the spotlight, speak barely a word to the audience and spin out one teenage passion play after another.' That's enough."

"Gee, you've got a wonderful memory," she said.

Corrigan nodded. "About things I'm interested in."

He handed her the earphones and Walkman. "Here, why don't you listen for a while."

Freda would have preferred listening to Corrigan. He seemed gentle and wise. She couldn't imagine him bombing anything.

Donaldson asked Jefferson, the FBI man with the pilot's license (private), to occupy the co-pilot's seat. McCoy, in his flight engineer seat, looked wan.

Over the cabin speaker came McCabe's voice. The chief exec sounded tense. "Ron, trouble. Real trouble."

Donaldson took a deep breath and waited.

"Interpol sent a woman out to talk to Julia Guedet, the radiologist who seemed so cozy with Corrigan and his partner in Omaha. Here's her story in a nutshell:

"She had an affair with Corrigan and the partner. Corrigan was sexually jealous of the partner, although Corrigan gets most of the action. She isn't too sure the assault-suicide business was really like it seems and hints that maybe Corrigan might have bumped off Donovan because of his jealous feelings. She thinks Corrigan may be cuckoo.

"Five days ago Corrigan flies to Frankfurt and drops in on Julia unexpectedly. He wants to marry her! She says no sir, buddy, but is nice to him, shows him around Frankfurt, goes to bed with him.

"Now get this. She works for the security people at the Air Force base near Frankfurt. Guess what her job is? Trying to figure ways to detect new high-powered explosives. That's where her radiology background came into it. Also, probably a technical whiz kid.

"You won't believe it. She shows Corrigan her lab! Explosives and all! She lets him make a phone call from her lab office while she runs an errand—alone with some new explosives." McCabe rarely raised his voice, but it was raised now.

"Dig this. Corrigan placed the call—assuming there was one—at about noon yesterday, Friday, the day before the flight. He said he wanted to confirm his flight reservation, but I have my doubts. Remember, the bomb caller spoke perfect German and Corrigan speaks perfect German.

"Know what I think? I think Corrigan was the guy on the phone. I think Corrigan was the man who made the bomb threat. Remember the cargo handler who took the call? Said he heard planes taking off in the background over the phone. If Corrigan called from the base just south of the Frankfurt airport—where Julia's lab is—the cargo handler would have heard planes taking off. It's rush hour at the Frankfurt airport."

The cockpit was silent as a monastery. Finally, Donaldson said, "Do we know whether Corrigan took any of the explosives?"

"According to the Interpol babe who interrogated Julia in her apartment, Julia hadn't checked to find out. They're on the way to her lab at this minute. They'll find out. Then we'll know for certain."

McCabe paused. "Ron, I think I already know for certain. Corrigan is a nut. He stole some plastic. He has it with him on the plane. He made the bomb threat. He found some way to warn the other passengers not to fly. Right now he's sitting back in your beautiful 747 waiting for the bomb to go off."

Donaldson remembered Francis Moore, the detective in Omaha who interviewed the Western Auto employee. "I guess it fits, John. Corrigan liked to play chicken with trains as a kid. Now he's grown up. He likes to play chicken with airplanes."

"I see some hope there, John. People who play chicken aren't asking to die. They're just risking death. Corrigan may just be risking death. This means there's a chance that the bomb will go off—and a chance that it won't."

"You know how to brighten a fellow's day," Donaldson said.

The first thing Donaldson did was descend the plane to 10,000 feet, clearing with control. He would remain at this altitude until landing at Dulles. At 10,000 feet, the cabin would be depressurized. A bomb caused less damage in a depressurized cabin.

The next thing Donaldson did was call the purser. He hoped he wouldn't hear a lecture. He would have preferred calling his wife Susan, but she was in the upper deck lounge sobering up a co-pilot.

The purser appeared at the cockpit door. "Another medical emergency, captain?"

"Not medical. Maybe an emergency. Do you know of any attendants who have a pilot's license?"

The purser thought a minute. "Randy in cabin C is taking flying lessons. I don't think he has a license yet. Why?"

"Ask Randy to come see me."

The purser started to ask why again, but saw Donaldson's face and decided to do what he was told.

Donaldson said, "Don't mention this to anybody. Just Randy. I don't want to scare anyone, including you. We're in no difficulty. Not with the airplane."

The purser left and a minute later a handsome attendant with yellow hair appeared at the door.

"Can I help?"

"You can. Jefferson," he said to the FBI man in the co-pilot's uniform, sitting in the co-pilot's seat, "go back and bring Corrigan up . . ." He had to think a minute about where ". . . to the business section, right by the upper deck stairs. Sit with him. There's a phone on the bulkhead in front of the seat. I'll call you in a minute."

"Randy," he said. "You're now the co-pilot. Congratulations."

Randy's hazel eyes were wide but not with fear. He knew a challenge when he saw one.

"Jefferson," Donaldson said on the interphone. "Let me talk to the passenger."

"Corrigan," he said. "We know everything. Or almost everything.

We've talked to Julia. We know about the plastic in the lab. Right now we're checking to see if some is missing. If there is, Dr. Corrigan, you are in very hot water. We all are. Do you have anything to say?"

"If I did," Corrigan said, "I'm sure you wouldn't believe me. I take the fifth."

Donaldson asked to talk to Jefferson and said, "Jefferson, ask someone to bring his carry-on and jacket up to where you are sitting. Go through them very, very carefully. Then have a couple of attendants babysit Corrigan while you go back to cabin D where he was sitting. Get some crew to help. Search overhead bins, seats, life jackets under the seats, everything in a broad area around where he sat. Plus the lavatories—all the lavatories he might have used. Particularly the refuse bins. This has to be the most careful search you've ever conducted and the fastest. For the next hour and a half—until we're on the ground at Dulles—consider the plane and all of us in the gravest danger."

Donaldson paused. "I don't know what we're looking for. Have you ever seen plastic?"

"I've seen plastic," Jefferson said, possibly offended.

"Well, there won't be much of it. A tiny amount. Something new and powerful. Might fit in an ashtray with room left over." He added, "By the way, the guy's got a personal stereo. Check that out too."

"What else?" Jefferson asked. "When you find the time," Donaldson said, "have a heart to heart talk with this guy. It won't do any good, but really go at him."

Donaldson added, "And then do a body search. We'll try to find a rubber glove for you." Donaldson knew there probably wasn't one on the plane. He hoped Jefferson was not squeamish.

"Ron?" McCabe was again on the cockpit speaker. "I was right."

"Glad to hear it," said Donaldson, who was about to experience the stark terror pilots are supposed to experience every hundred years.

"A small piece of the plastic is missing. Very small, but enough to blow a large hole in your plane. Something else is missing."

Donaldson waited.

"The detonator," McCabe said.

"Oh yes, the detonator. A kitchen timer?"

"Fancier than that. A cassette tape. The 1812 Overture. When the cannons go off at the end, the bomb goes off. A beautifully designed harmonic signal."

"Hang on," Donaldson said. "Let me ask the FBI man something."

He called Jefferson on the interphone.

"Find anything on Corrigan?"

"Nothing."

"Not surprised. Have you gone through his carry-on?"

"Yup. Nothing."

"Are there cassette tapes in his carry-on?"

"Two of them."

Donaldson swallowed hard. "What's on the cassettes?"

"Country western singer. Roy Orbison."

"Look in the Sony," Donaldson said.

"Jefferson looked. "More Orbison," he said.

"Goddammit," said Donaldson. "Go back, round up the crew. Look everywhere for a cassette tape.

"Any particular cassette tape?"

"Yes. Look for a tape of the 1812 Overture. If you find it, clutch it in your hot little hand and say a prayer."

Twenty-five minutes later, Jefferson called Donaldson. "Still no plastic. No cassette tape. Why don't airplanes come supplied with plastic gloves?"

Freda Van Valkenburg had been in the lavatory when Jefferson told the crew a cassette of the 1812 Overture was now on the search list. She came out and resumed looking for plastic.

An hour of searching produced nothing. A few attendants were desultarily poking around seat covers as far away as first class, where Corrigan had never been seen to go.

Freda was sitting back in section D. At first she had been frightened, but now felt calm. She felt they were wrong to suspect the nice passenger who liked Roy Orbison. A little bored, she opened her purse and removed her own personal stereo—a Toshiba. She opened the flap and inserted the cassette that Corrigan had loaned her. She put on the earphones, punched

100

a button on the Toshiba, closed her eyes and waited peacefully for the flight to end.

She recognized the music right away.

They were 30 minutes out of Dulles when Jefferson, walking back through the cabin, saw Freda wearing earphones connected to a Sony (the agent didn't know Sony's from Toshiba's). He stopped and gazed at her. Suddenly his heart did a flip-flop.

"My God, honey, what are you listening to?"

She pushed back one earphone from her left ear.

"I'm sorry. What did you ask?"

"What are you listening to?"

She told him and he lurched toward her. He grabbed the Sony/Toshiba from her lap and fumbled with the buttons. He found the stop button and the whirring sound stopped.

Freda looked at him in amazement. She was enjoying the Overture. It was about over. The cannons would go off any minute.

14

Dulles

Donaldson had never heard of landing a 747 solo! He had no choice. His co-pilot had been drinking and was under surveillance in the lounge. His flight engineer was sitting where he should be, but doubled up in pain. Sitting in the co-pilot's seat was a flight attendant whose only qualification was that he was paying to take flying lessons.

He could land the plane alone—he was sure of it. Why, then, was he anxious? If something went wrong, there was Susan, the other crew, the FBI agent whom he'd come to like, and a passenger who might or might not deserve to live. In fact, their fate might still rest with the passenger. They had found the detonator-cassette in the nick of time. But maybe the bastard had something up his sleeve. An odd one. Sitting in a middle seat in section B, the FBI agent on one side, the heftiest male attendant on the other, three other attendants sitting behind. An island of calmness in a sea of blue uniforms. Unperturbed. Enjoying himself. Thinking about it, Donaldson felt a wave of nausea.

Then there was the plane. Donaldson had a romance with the 747, more so than with any plane he had flown. He could hardly bear the idea that the huge graceful machine—one of the great engineering achievements in history—was as vulnerable as Susan and himself and all people everywhere.

They were approaching Nantucket. The lower clouds scattered, giving a clear view of the Cape Cod hook. Donaldson knew the island well; the season was well underway. The eastern tip of Long Island came into view, dotted with sport-sailing fleets. Power boats laid down arcs of frothy wake, some with skiers in close trail. A placid, early summer day was below.

Donaldson continued coaching Randy on handling the radio. In time he would be able to lower the wheels and position the wing flaps.

"Christ, here I am, 17 hours in a Cessna 152, and I'm a 747 co-pilot. Will you sign my log book for this time, Ron?"

Donaldson wished he had not said Ron, but didn't mention it. Instead, he was jovial.

"Hell yes, Randy. If we didn't have everyone but the Marine Band greeting us, I'd give you the landing."

Kennedy Traffic Control called. "TA 131, I understand you want an expedited approach for Dulles. We'll be handing you off to Washington control early. They're advised."

Donaldson nodded to Randy. "Thank them."

"Thanks, Kennedy. TA 131." Randy grinned as he hung up the microphone.

Donaldson sensed Randy settling in, more at ease. He pointed out Fire Island on the south shore of Long Island and JFK coming into view beyond. "Making Canarsie approaches today at Kennedy," he commented. "Hell of an approach!"

"Yeah, I know. Not many captains like all the circling to get around landing southeast." Now, Randy really felt like a part of the cockpit crew. The chatter was just like he had heard on his brief trips to the cockpit with coffee for the crew.

"I'll never forget an Aeroflot pilot bitching about the Canarsie approach one night," Donaldson said. "He came around for a second attempt after missing his first approach, and again he didn't get lined up for the landing and had to pull up. He came on the radio and told the tower, 'Dat approach is for da shits, ve go to Boston.' Really broke everyone up."

The brief quiet was interrupted. "TA 131, this is Kennedy Control. Change over to Washington Control on 123.7 megacycles for further clearance. Have a good day. Happy landing."

"Thanks, Kennedy, and good day," Randy responded without coaching. "Guess they're speeding us up," he murmured as he dialed 123.7 on the radio.

Donaldson decided to review the landing for Randy before they got into the traffic at Dulles.

"Randy, you have the radio okay. Now I want to review the landing. I'll call for the flap settings when I want to slowdown. Just pull the lever to the notch that I call for—five degrees, ten degrees and so forth." Randy practiced grasping the flap handle beside the throttle.

"The landing gear is simple," Donaldson continued. "Simple if you watch for the warning lights sequencing and finally get them all green with the gear level down and locked." It didn't sound simple to Randy. He moved his left hand to the round wheel-like lever in front of his left knee projecting from the instrument panel.

"Now, for the landing," Donaldson said with more emphasis. "Forget the Cessna. It touches down with your eye level five feet from the runway. Just sitting on the ground in a 747, you're 35 feet in the air." Randy nodded, his confidence ebbing.

"On landing," Donaldson continued, "the gear will touch on—tail down, nose high—with you and me in the cockpit some 55 feet above the runway."

"I know. Unbelievable."

"You'll feel like we're going to fly low over the airport and miss the field entirely and then the wheels will squeak on," Donaldson said. "It takes a little experience to overcome the feeling of still being five stories high on landings."

"Can't wait," Randy said.

Descent for landing would start after Atlantic City, changing over to Washington Air Traffic Control Center. Ordinarily the flight engineer would be making his final write-up in the log book and talking with the Dulles ramp office for his arrival advisories. McCoy wasn't up to it; they would be landing without these amenities.

The pre-landing checklist would be read by Randy. Other essentials at the flight engineer's station would be done by Donaldson.

"Never was a flight engineer," Donaldson said, almost apologetically. "Started out as a co-pilot on DC-3s, then checked out as a captain and got used to engineers when we got the Connies. Great bunch. Good help, but easy for pilots to get lazy on the systems. Now, I'd better double-check the items Mac would usually check."

"Sorry I can't help much there, Skipper." Randy was getting the hang of the language, though still unfamiliar with the nuances.

"You're doing fine. Good thing Boeing set things up for landings without a lot of monitoring the engineer panel."

Donaldson nudged his seat on the curved track back and to the left so he could slice into Mac's seat. Mac had moved back to the lounge to lie down on the floor; the pain had become unbearable, even for Mac. Donaldson picked up the checklist and read aloud:

"Cabin pressure: set 200 feet below airport level." This protected cabin pressure until the landing gear was planted on the runway.

"Fuel pumps: all on, and cross feeds open. Same for low fuel landings. No problem.

"Tank selectors: all set tank to engine. Simple enough. That looks like the major items. Should be set if nothing else comes up."

Rising from the engineer's seat, Donaldson slipped back into his own seat, wondering how Mac was doing.

"This is your captain," he said over the intercom. "That's the Potomac we're passing over. The nation's capitol is in plain view ahead on our left. We'll be landing in 10 minutes." For a moment he had forgotten the scene in the cabin. He hoped the attendants would think he was kidding instead of absent-minded, or bananas.

Eight minutes out.

"TA 131, this is Dulles Tower. Have you on radar over Godfrey's Farm. Wind is 210 degrees at eight knots. Delta 757 departing. You're cleared to land on runway 19 left."

Randy acknowledged the clearance, craning his neck for a view of the gently rolling terrain; a lush green with a patchwork of white railed fences enclosing the estates of the Virginia horsey set.

Randy waited for the down gear command. It came. He grasped the gear lever with a death-like grip, pulled out, then pushed down. The three clusters of lights flickered, a mild thump was felt, a whirring, straining sound lasted for eight to ten seconds, then another slight thump, and the three lights on the instrument panel flashed a steady green.

Randy was transfixed at the chain reaction resulting from his response to Donaldson's command. "Gear down and three green lights," Randy announced, trying to conceal a feeling of pride.

❦

Donaldson could have merely observed the approach and touched down with hands off. He opted to land hands on.

In fact, the entire flight from Frankfurt could have been conducted on automatic pilot: the climb, the cruise, the routing and navigation, descent, approach and landing. After touchdown, he would have had to taxi manually to the parking area. For most of the flight, he sometimes felt as irrelevant as the early astronauts watching the planet spin under them.

Air speed 155 knots, reduced gradually to 147 knots (169 statute miles per hour) for crossing the runway boundary. Speeds were determined by landing weight plus 30 percent above stall speed. The descent rate was 700 feet per minute, reduced by one-half, 500 feet above the runway.

Breaking silence, Donaldson said, "Secret to a good landing is to get the bird down to two inches off the runway and then hold it off."

Randy frowned, trying to visualize inches when he was still working on several feet from the runway in landing Cessnas. Then he realized it was preposterous and Donaldson had cracked a little joke.

The plane was now over the approach end of the runway. Touchdown was 1,500 feet ahead. Donaldson gently coaxed the yoke another two inches into his midsection. The nose raised higher, the far end of the runway barely visible. He scanned air speed, sink rate, runway center line and now radio altimeter, which read 90 feet, 80 feet, 60 feet—back slightly on the yoke, 40, 30, 20, 10 feet and sscheerpp—touchdown!

"Hope no one spilled their coffee," Donaldson said.

Reverse thrust was slowly applied. Dulles had plenty of runway for jumbos.

"Welcome home, TA 131," was the first comment from the tower operator. "The follow-me vehicle is on your right at the high-speed turnoff. He'll lead you to the security area for parking."

As TA 131 taxied westerly, the sun loomed, now on the horizon, a deep orange hue by contrast to the glistening annoyance it had been for the crossing. Dusk was dulling the colorful countryside.

Dulles airport's terminal building was the work of Eero Sarrinen, the Finnish architect. Frank Lloyd Wright would probably have liked it. Not a box with a top. No squares. Rather, its curved structured emulated nature.

106

A parabolic-designed roof seemed to float above the open glass sidewalls.

TA 131 passed in view on the distant south taxiway for the isolated security area.

❦

McCabe, Vice President for Flight Operations, had no trouble catching a plane from LaGuardia to Dulles. The total trip, including a helicopter hop from the Pan Am building, took 40 minutes.

Waiting on the tarmac, he saw TA 131 approach from the northeast. The landing was smooth. All the stress Donaldson had undergone on the flight obviously hadn't interfered with his ability to make a silky-smooth landing. At the time, McCabe didn't know Donaldson had made the landing alone, or almost alone.

Stairs were wheeled up to the plane's flank and the left front door opened. A male flight attendant descended. Behind him was a small man in a business suit, wearing a large hat. The FBI agent dressed as a co-pilot followed him. Then came Donaldson.

The plane had been parked in a secure area. Two fire trucks were positioned close by, their helmeted and rubber-suited crews standing alongside. With McCabe were three FBI agents and four uniformed policemen.

"Hello, John," Donaldson said to McCabe. He introduced Randy the attendant, and Jefferson in his co-pilot's disguise.

The attendant looked fresh. Jefferson, the experienced FBI man, looked exhausted. Then Donaldson introduced the passenger. "Mr. McCabe, Dr. Corrigan."

McCabe stared at him. "So, you're the problem," he said.

The man smiled. "Nice to meet you. If I've been a problem, I apologize." He impressed McCabe as a mild-mannered even keel, little man with a Midwestern accent. He wore a gray business suit, his tie neatly knotted. The cowboy hat was much too large for his narrow face.

"Well, come with us," McCabe said, and the group moved off to a hangar-like building a dozen yards away. The last crew member was just leaving the plane. McCoy was holding his back with one hand and gesturing with the other while a doctor listened. There was a nurse in white standing next to Lois Lister. The majestic 747 loomed ominously over the Lilliputians moving about on the ground in the Washington dusk. The time was 8:33.

107

McCabe, his friend Donaldson and three FBI agents sat side by side facing Corrigan across the table. He had been strip-searched one more time, using the bathroom across the hall. His large brown bag was open, with the clothes neatly folded and returned, except for the arm of a striped pajama top dangling from the side. His carry-on had been emptied on the table: shaving kit, a paperback mystery, aspirin, the Sony Walkman, two Orbison cassettes. The 1812 Overture was also on the table, a few feet away.

The interrogation had been broken by long silences. There was no good guy, bad guy routine. Corrigan seemed somewhat distracted, answering questions as if his mind were elsewhere. He seemed completely relaxed. His answers were polite but short; he never elaborated, he never volunteered information. His deportment very much resembled that of a forensic psychiatrist testifying as an expert witness in a jury trial. He was there to help, but neutral in all matters.

A bald-headed man in a plaid sportcoat came in the room and sat next to McCabe. "Tom Frederickson," he said. "Federal DA's office." Everyone nodded except Corrigan.

"Mr. Corrigan," he said. "Doctor," someone corrected. "I'm going to read you your rights, then review what we know."

From the beginning, it was clear Frederickson knew everything, or at least everything McCabe and Donaldson and Interpol and detective Moore in Omaha knew. He dwelled most on the visit to Julia's lab. He asked again and again about the plastic. Again and again Corrigan denied stealing plastic. He was asked about the cassette. The cassette was his, he said. He had brought it with him from Omaha.

Finally, Frederickson gave up. "I don't think any of us believes you, Dr. Corrigan, but we can't prove anything. We'll call your wife, see if she can verify that the tape was yours. I personally doubt that it is. Meanwhile, you'll be held in custody as a suspect. A judge tomorrow will decide what to charge."

"A suspect?"

"Dr. Corrigan, we have no idea what your motives are. You may be— what should I say?—disturbed. Putting it bluntly, plain nuts. All we know is that there is overwhelming circumstantial evidence that you stole highly explosive plastic from a laboratory in Frankfurt and the cassette that detonates it. The cassette is there on the table. We don't know what you did with the plastic."

"I have a suggestion," McCabe said. "Dr. Corrigan, would you be willing to listen to the 1812 Overture? All the way through?"

Corrigan fiddled with the brim of his cowboy hat. He looked off to the side and smiled. "Why not?"

The others looked at McCabe as if he has lost his mind. Frederickson said, "Sir, wouldn't that be . . . dangerous?"

"Why?" McCabe said. "We've searched him and everything he's got. There's no bomb here, no plastic. The plane's out of range, granting the possibility that a bomb is there no one found."

The others looked at each other. A couple shrugged. "I think it's a good idea," Corrigan said. "You say I stole a cassette. I say I brought it from home. If I listen to it—when nothing happens—wouldn't that help my case?"

"Let him listen to it somewhere else," an FBI agent said. "Somewhere bomb proof. Why take a chance? Wait till tomorrow. Get advice from a bomb specialist."

Donaldson said, "Look, I just crossed the Atlantic with this man. I talked with him at length. Mr. Jefferson talked with him at length. I want to know now. I don't want to wait. There's no bomb around—we all agree. Let him listen to it."

No one said anything. Donaldson continued, "I'll make a bet with anyone here. Corrigan is bluffing. He likes to play chicken, we know that, but if that tape is a detonator, he won't listen to it. Not all the way through. Because he won't absolutely be sure. He's hopped on the train. That's fine, but he wants to hop off safely."

Not everyone there knew what Donaldson was referring to, but there seemed to be a change in sentiment.

"Okay," Frederickson said. "This may turn out to be the best confession we're going to get. He's a cool customer. But tomorrow, God knows what story he'll have."

"Go on," Donaldson said. "Put on your earphones." He handed the Sony to Corrigan. "Plug 'em in. Turn it on. Listen."

Corrigan did as he was told.

The 1812 Overture has four movements and lasts 35 minutes. There was a clock on the wall. As Corrigan sat passively with the earphones on, every man in the room studied the clock.

The minute hand had moved 31 minutes and 43 seconds when Corrigan abruptly removed the earphone and pushed the stop button on the Sony.

He leaned back in the chair and looked at the men across the table. He stretched and yawned.

Then he pushed the cowboy hat across the table in McCabe's direction.

"Someplace you forgot to look," he said.

The men across the table gasped more or less in unison. McCabe tentatively picked up the hat. He looked in the crown. He reached in and peeled back the hat's satin lining. He stared inside as if in a trance. "Here it is," he said.

Corrigan said, "Are you happy now?"

Epilogue

They left the plastic in the cowboy hat and placed the hat in a large open field. They played the 1812 Overture all the way through. At the end of the final movement the cannons went off. The hat exploded, leaving a crater about three feet deep and five feet wide. Everyone was impressed about how such a small amount of plastic—less than two ounces—could make such a big hole.

❦

Corrigan was transferred from jail to St. Elizabeth's Hospital in Washington for a psychiatric evaluation. He stayed six weeks, a model patient. Summarizing the evaluation:

The staff was split regarding Corrigan's diagnosis. Some were convinced he was a madman, a sociopath. Some thought such a nice man couldn't possibly commit a crime.

Holders of the first view were impressed by Corrigan's attention to detail, suggesting to them a calculating criminal mind. Other actions suggested he was careless, taking chances no ordinary criminal would take.

They spent hours discussing the shooting incident in Omaha. Lieutenant Moore of the Omaha PD flew to Washington and talked to the psychiatrists. He presented his theory: the painstaking preparations for shooting the partner and making it look like a suicide. Shooting himself in the abdomen, knowing the seriousness of the wound made the possibility of a hoax seem ludicrous. But first making sure the wound would also be unserious as possible. The elaborate X-ray tests to determine the exact position of the internal organs. The enema to reduce the chance of infection. Plotting the trajectory of the bullet with mathematical precision. Even arranging his clothes before he shot himself so the cloth wouldn't contaminate the wound and so he would know exactly where to shoot. Probably placing a tiny dot on his lower abdomen with a marking pen, which would be obliterated by the hole and powder burn. Possibly scrubbing the site with an alcohol sponge before shooting, although no alcohol or sponge was found on the scene. Then lying down outside the car—after he had killed Donovan—so he would be in the position in which the X-rays were taken earlier. Finally, using a .32 short with little penetrating power, not even enough to completely penetrate his back.

Attention to detail.

The psychiatrists pondered motives. Of course, there was the jealousy motive, making it a garden variety crime of passion. Or was it masochism? Did he want to be caught? No, that wasn't it, they said. He did everything not to be caught. Clearly he was not suicidal. He wasn't even homicidal in the usual sense. He just didn't care what happened. For days and years he led a quiet ordinary nice guy life until he couldn't stand it any longer. He needed to break the routine, take a wild gamble. He needed the thrill. The thrill was the thing. If he got away with it, wonderful. If he didn't, well, so it goes. He didn't care. If there is a caring center in the brain that makes one concerned about what happens to one's self or others, he lacked it. A flaw. Probably genetic.

He was a magnificent deceiver. He kept the flaw hidden from everyone. Only Julia—and possibly Jerry Herzog— suspected it. But when the time came to play chicken, he couldn't resist.

This was the Russian roulette theory.

Julia? Who could say? The sexual attraction was probably real. Maybe he loved her in his way. Maybe it was just more chicken: checking in his hometown hotel, daring people to recognize him. Sex in his office with the door unlocked. Asking to be caught, asking for his Gentleman Jim persona to come apart, asking to be unmasked Not wanting disaster. Not caring.

In hindsight, the psychiatrists decided, Corrigan wasn't as smart as he was unstable. "I think when all is said and done," one commented, "we're all going to see that Bob Corrigan thought because he was such a great guy, and everybody who knew him thought he was such a great guy, no one would ever really believe he was capable of doing what he did."

When Corrigan learned he was going to be extradited to Omaha to face murder charges, he lost his cool, just for a minute. He talked about the Frankfurt affair and confessed.

He had called in the bomb threat from Julia's office when he was supposed to be confirming his reservations and she was on an errand. He accompanied her back to her apartment and then left, saying he wanted to do some shopping. He caught a cab to the airport. Here was the most amazing thing: he persuaded a TA supervisor at the check-in counter that he was FBI and needed a copy of the passenger list. Everyone agreed he would have made a great actor; he came over so genuine that the supervisor didn't ask for an ID.

For the next eight hours—almost until midnight—he called the passengers on the list: those who had reconfirmed their flight and left numbers where they could be reached (most had, it turned out). Using a hotel public booth, he plugged in coin after coin to reach the passengers or at least leave a message. It didn't take long as it might seem. His message was simple: the plane will be bombed.

At this point the Feds would have taken over, but the State of Nebraska prevailed. Corrigan would be extradited to Omaha.

The Omaha jury took two days to reach a verdict. The clincher—the prosecutors later agreed—were the bullets.

Two had been fired. If you believed Corrigan, the first bullet had been fired at him. It had been fired by Donovan before he fired the second bullet, shooting himself.

The ballistic expert said Corrigan's version didn't fit the evidence. He had examined the two cartridges. One had been tampered with—there were pliers marks on the rim. The other showed no signs of tampering.

The slug that entered Donovan and killed him came from the untampered shell. It had penetrated his heart and exited through the thick muscles of his back, punching a deep hole in the car seat.

The slug that hit Corrigan came from the tampered cartridge. The tampering suggested the slug had been removed before the bullet had been fired, suggesting, perhaps that some powder had been removed from the cartridge, reducing its power to penetrate. If this was the bullet that struck Corrigan, it would explain why the slug had not totally penetrated his body but had lodged lazily in his back muscle.

It was clear from the placement of the cartridges in the pistol's chamber that the untampered bullet—the one that shot Corrigan—was the second bullet fired.

It supported Moore's theory that Corrigan had shot the partner, killing him, and then shot himself for an alibi.

Guilty of first. Corrigan got a life sentence.

Note About Explosives

For explosive buffs—the benign kind—some information provided by an FBI explosives expert about how a cassette tape can detonate plastic may be informative.

Nobody paid any attention to it but attached to the band on Corrigan's hat was a small wooden ornament—a replica of a Texas longhorn steer—of the type that commonly decorates cowboy hats. Corrigan had found in Julia's lab a tiny microphone, the size of a pea, with tiny wires coming out the back. He knew instantly what it was for. He removed the ornament with his pen knife carved out a hole in the backside that would accommodate a pea-sized microphone. He ran the tiny wires up a seam in the inside of the hat, inserting them into microcondenser, smaller than a pea, lodged in the plastic. A condenser is like a battery, except it generates only a single electrical discharge.

The detonator worked by converting sound into electrical energy. The cannons in the 1812 Overture have a very low frequency of a specific wave length. The microphone was designed to respond only to this specific wave length. The chances that other noise in most environments—such as an airplane cabin—would slip through the "frequency window" in the microphone were infinitesimally small.

When the microphone "recognized" the cannons, an electrical signal was sent to the microcondenser, which discharged a larger electrical impulse into the plastic—sufficient to make it explode.

The FBI expert made a point that this was an extremely complicated and unreliable way to detonate a bomb. For example, the cassette would have to be played an exact distance from the microphone and be played at a particular high volume to produce sufficient voltage to penetrate the outer shell of the ornament. Through trial and error, the exact distance and volume to detonate Corrigan's hat were determined. The chances of the device not working were very great. The FBI expert opined that only an idiot, although a clever idiot, would consider designing such a device. There were many other well-known devices for detonating bombs that are infinitely easier to manufacture and infinitely more reliable.

The FBI agent also commented on the dynamite trick (chapter eight). If a circle of dynamite sticks are parallel wired and explode simultaneously, a person inside the circle would not be harmed because the force would hit him exactly from all sides. The body is like a bag of fluid—push in from all sides and nothing happens. He compared it to scuba diving, where water pressure can exert a tremendous force but the diver is unharmed because the force is equal from all sides (this may not, however, prevent bubbles forming in the blood and lungs). The FBI expert considered the dynamite trick dangerous in the extreme. If the dynamite sticks failed to explode simultaneously—and the chances were good that they wouldn't—the person in the center would be blown to pieces. Even if the trick worked, the noise would likely shatter his eardrums. Plugs in the ear and closing the mouth would reduce the risk somewhat, but not entirely. The FBI agent asked his listeners whether Corrigan was hard of hearing. Nobody had noticed it.

The FBI agent concluded his comments by observing that Corrigan, in his opinion, was either very crazy or very stupid to play around with such dangerous toys.